CAR RACING

Titles in the History of Sports series include:
Baseball
Basketball
Boxing
Cycling
Football
Golf
Hockey
Skiing
Soccer
Swimming
Tennis
Track and Field
Volleyball
Wrestling

CAR RACING

BY MARTHA CAPWELL FOX

LUCENT
BOOKS ®

THOMSON
———— ✦ ————™
GALE

San Diego • Detroit • New York • San Francisco • Cleveland • New Haven, Conn. • Waterville, Maine • London • Munich

On cover: Driver Jeff Gordon celebrates his victory at the 2001 Southern 500 race in Darlington, South Carolina.

© 2004 by Lucent Books. Lucent Books is an imprint of The Gale Group, Inc.,
a division of Thomson Learning, Inc.

Lucent Books® and Thomson Learning™ are trademarks used herein under license.

For more information, contact
Lucent Books
27500 Drake Rd.
Farmington Hills, MI 48331-3535
Or you can visit our Internet site at http://www.gale.com

LIBRARY OF CONGRESS CATALOGING-IN-PUBLICATION DATA

Fox, Martha Capwell.
    Car racing / by Martha Capwell Fox.
        p. cm. — (History of sports)
Summary: Discusses the origins and evolution of the sport of auto racing, as well as mem-
orable events and key personalities in the sport's history.
Includes bibliographical references and index.
    ISBN 1-59018-354-1 (hardback : alk. paper)
    1. Automobile racing—Juvenile literature. 2. Automobile racing—United States—
Juvenile literature. [1. Automobile racing.] I. Title. II. Series.
    GV1029.13.F69 2004
    796.72—dc22
                                                                              2003016248

Contents

FOREWORD

More than many areas of human endeavor, sports give us the opportunity to see the possibilities in our physical selves. As participants, we all too quickly find limits to how fast we can run, how high we can jump, how far and straight we can hit a golf ball. But as spectators we can surpass those limits as we view the accomplishments of others and see how fast, how smooth, and how strong a human being can be. We marvel at the gravity-defying leaps of a Michael Jordan as he strains towards a basketball hoop or at the dribbling of a Mia Hamm as she eludes defenders on the soccer field. We shake our heads in disbelief at the talents of a young Tiger Woods hitting an approach shot to the green or the speed of a Carl Lewis as he appears to glide around an Olympic track.

These are what the sports media call "the oohs and ahhs" of sports—the stuff of highlight reels and *Sports Illustrated* covers. But to understand a sport only in the context of its most artistic modern athletes is shortsighted, for it does little justice to the accomplishments of the athletes or to the sport itself. Far more wise is to view a sport as a continuum—a constantly moving, evolving process. On this continuum are not only the superstars of today, but the people who first played the sport, who thought about rules and strategies that would make it more challenging to play as well as a delight to watch.

Lucent Books' series, the History of Sports, provides such a continuum. Each book explores the development of a sport from its basic roots onward, and tries to answer questions that a reader might wonder about. Who were its first players, and what sorts of rules did the sport have then? What kinds of equipment were used in the beginning and what changes have taken place over the years?

Each title in the History of Sports also identifies key individuals in the sport's history—people whose leadership or skills have made a difference in the way the sport is played today. Included will be the easily recognized names, the Mia Hamms and the Sammy Sosas, the Wilt Chamberlains and the Wilma Rudolphs. But there are also the names of past greats, people like baseball's King Kelly, soccer's Sir Stanley Matthews, and basketball's Hank Luisetti—who may be less familiar today, but were as synonymous with their sports at one time as the "oohs and ahhs" players of today.

Finally, the series looks at the aspects of a sport that are particularly important in its current point on the continuum. Baseball today is better understood knowing about salary caps and union negotiators. One cannot truly know modern soccer without knowing about the specter of fan violence at matches. And learning about the role of instant replay is critical to a thorough understanding of today's professional football games. In viewing a sport as a continuum, the strides that have been made along the way are that much more admirable. It is a richer view, and one that shows how yesterday's limits have been surpassed—and how the limits of today are the possibilities of athletes in the future.

"Gentlemen, Start Your Engines"

No one is exactly sure when the first auto race was held, but doubtless it happened shortly after the second car was built. Another safe assumption is that it was held in Europe, where self-propelled vehicles first hit the road near the end of the nineteenth century. The earliest races focused mostly on endurance—a drive of twenty to thirty miles was a major feat for the first cars. However, the desire to prove that an auto was faster and more powerful than its competitors quickly became *the* reason to race. Concerns about safety—for both drivers and spectators—followed hard on the heels of increased speeds.

Thus, by the turn of the twentieth century, the three most important factors in motor racing were already in place: power (which makes speed), durability, and safety. Over the years emphasis has shifted many times to one factor or another, but no single factor has been preeminent for long. Whether a race car was built by a huge consumer car company, a small shop dedicated only to racing, or a skilled amateur in a lonely garage, long-term success came only when each of the three major factors was built in.

The earliest races, in the 1890s, were over public roads that in Europe tended to be wide and well kept. This practice, which mimicked the European horse-racing practice of setting up temporary, overland racecourses, established a road racing tradition in Europe that continues to the present time. In the United States, however, the roads were poor and the oval track of horse racing was the norm. For this reason, fairly small, closed, oval tracks quickly created a uniquely American form of racing that began to be exported to the rest of the world only in the past decade, with mixed results. Nevertheless, after little more than one hundred years, auto racing in all of its forms is the world's biggest spectator sport.

American writer Robert F. Jones calls this obsession with car racing "The virus of velocity,"[1] The urge to be the first and the fastest has always been a human im-

pulse. It has obviously been a driving force since the first days of racing—but not the only one.

Though traditionalists bemoan the commercialism of the twenty-first century's television-dominated racing, the truth is that selling cars was one of the first major reasons to race. Though they were not plastered with logos and advertising decals, even the earliest racers were prominently identified with their maker—Ford, Mercedes, Alfa Romeo, Chevrolet, and Fiat. Some carmakers used racing as a way to tout the superiority of their machines;

Thousands of fans pack the stands at Michigan International Speedway. Car racing is the world's most popular spectator sport.

some, to test new innovations; others went racing to raise the money to build mass-market cars. NASCAR may have brought the phrase "Win on Sunday, sell on Monday" into the vocabulary, but the concept existed in Europe and America fifty years earlier.

Racing and car manufacturing have had a kind of symbiotic relationship from the start. Literally thousands of automotive innovations—ranging from fuel injection to disc brakes to independent suspensions to front wheel drive to seat belts, and including small mechanical improvements the average driver is oblivious to, such as multiple valves and overhead cams—were first developed for race cars. Carmakers learned a lot on racetracks—and still do—about making cars safer, more reliable, more efficient, and faster. Tire manufacturers do the same, as do fuel refiners, lubricant synthesizers, helmet designers, and seat-belt engineers. The racetrack is their laboratory and their quality control system. The cars that carry the world's people and goods would be very different if there had not been racing.

Though technical advances have made racing safer, especially since the 1970s, auto racing has undeniably been fraught with tragedy. It should be remembered, though, that far fewer people have died during racing's 110 year history than are killed in one year on America's roads.

Ironically, advances in racing technology that produce sudden spikes in speed have often caused terrible runs of accidents and deaths. One such period was the late 1960s and early 1970s, when track configurations and safety provisions lagged behind the tremendous jumps in speed. There have been many times in racing history when the human death toll became so high that there were calls to ban racing. For instance, after the catastrophic 1955 Le Mans race in France when a Mercedes plowed into a trackside crowd and killed eighty-three spectators, many European races were canceled and Mercedes withdrew from racing for more than twenty-five years.

In most cases the people associated with motor sports have used the lessons learned from crashes, deaths, and injuries to try to ensure that a tragedy will not be repeated. Others seek to break through technological barriers to push the limits of speed, power, and efficiency even further. They are driven solely by the desire to design and produce the perfect machine and might even be perfectly happy never to see their creations on a racetrack. Such automotive ascetics exist, but they are a tiny minority among racing folk. The rest—drivers, crew, engineers, fans—are drawn by the speed, the sound, the smell, and the sheer physical and emotional exhilaration of racing. In their minds no other sport can deliver that thrill.

CHAPTER 1

Open Wheel Racing

American open wheel racing is the oldest motor-racing championship in the world. It has always been the premier event of on-track speed, racing technology, and driver expertise in U.S. racing. The open wheel (which means open cockpit) cars that raced at the Indianapolis 500 race became the standard for American motor racing until after World War II when stock car and drag racing began in earnest. Even the generic name, Indy car, which was used until the late 1990s to describe both the highest level of open wheel racing, and the cars that raced in it, paid homage to open wheel racing's pinnacle. (Now, however, that term is copyrighted and jealously held by the Indianapolis Motor Speedway, and may be used only to describe the race cars that compete in the Indy Racing League.) Almost all technological improvements in racing motors, tires, brakes, and steering assemblies in American race cars sprang from the desire to be in first place at the end of Indy's five hundred miles.

Indianapolis: The Greatest Spectacle in Racing

American auto racing was still young when the first Indianapolis 500 was held on May 30, 1911. As in Europe the very first car races in the United States, held in the 1890s, were open-road events. By 1900, however, there were also many county fair races, held on the same half-mile dirt tracks used for horse racing.

Ray Harroun, in his Marmon "Wasp," won the first Indianapolis 500 in 1911. Today, every car racer dreams of victory at the Indy 500.

Early race promoters quickly saw the financial advantages of these closed-circuit events: Spectators had to buy an admission ticket rather than just ramble across some open fields and find a place to watch by the side of the road. American fans quickly got used to being able to see the entire race, not just cars whizzing past once every fifteen minutes. And car manufacturers saw oval-track races as a way to focus all their attention—and the spectators'—on horsepower and speed rather than handling. This became the American "formula" for auto racing: high-powered cars on oval tracks.

American racing has always been closely tied to the auto manufacturers. In 1908, when a group of Indianapolis businessmen came up with the idea of a two-and-one-half-mile testing track for their city, the American auto industry was not entirely centered in Detroit; many cities were competing for a share of the car-building business. These businessmen thought that a national testing facility in Indianapolis would help clinch the car manufacturing title for their city. One of their group, Carl Fisher, was appointed to construct a track, and he bought 328 acres of farmland only four miles south of downtown Indianapolis.

Less than one year later, the Indianapolis Motor Speedway—two and one-half miles of gravel track surrounded by three miles of board fence, with more than twenty-five thousand grandstand seats, forty-one infield buildings, and three thousand hitching posts for horses—opened with the championship race of the Federation of American Motorcyclists. The track proved to be too big and too flat for motorcycle racing, but on August 19, 1909, a three-day auto racing event was held that launched the Speedway into fame.

On the first day Barney Oldfield, already a veteran racer, set a new world record for the mile—43.1 seconds, or 83.2 miles per hour. The next day 1908 national champion Louis Strang set a record for

one hundred miles: one hour and thirty-two minutes. The third day there were two races; the first, a 250-miler, saw five records reset by Barney Oldfield.

Despite the records these races are more remembered for the ensuing carnage. The gravel track had deteriorated badly during the first day's race, and two racers were killed in accidents caused by blinding dust. The second day was incident free, but during the third day's three-hundred-mile race, three people died in crashes—a mechanic and two spectators. Other spectators were seriously hurt. The race was stopped early, and the track owners, appalled by the death toll,

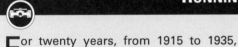

RUNNING ON WOOD

For twenty years, from 1915 to 1935, some of the best racing in America took place on wooden tracks. Twenty of the one-to-two-mile superspeedways were built of wooden beams two inches thick by four inches wide laid on edge; some of the tracks had turns banked as steeply as fifty-two degrees. On the board tracks the supercharged Miller and Duesenberg race engines of the mid-1920s ran thirty to thirty-five miles per hour faster than at the Brickyard. The inaugural race on the two-mile Chicago oval, on June 26, 1915, was a return match between Dario Resta and Ralph DePalma, who had finished second and first, respectively, at Indianapolis the previous month. On the bricks Resta had pushed DePalma to a new record average speed of 89.84 miles per hour; on the boards Resta ran a steady

97.58 against a strong field. Mechanical trouble took DePalma out early. The all-time board track record was set in 1926 on Atlantic City's 1.5-mile arena: Harry Hartz averaged 134 miles per hour in his Miller Special.

The speeds attracted huge crowds. The board tracks are generally credited with the tremendous increase in interest in auto racing that occurred in the 1920s. The twenty tracks were scattered all over the country—from New Hampshire to Florida, west through Iowa, Nebraska, and Kansas, to California and Washington. Wooden tracks were very expensive to maintain, however, and many located near big cities were soon overwhelmed by urban development. The depression ended most organized racing in the 1930s, and the wooden tracks vanished.

decided to resurface the track with bricks—3.2 million of them. The Brickyard, as the Indianapolis Motor Speedway is popularly known, was born.

Hear the Engines Roar for Five Hundred Miles

The brick paving was a wise decision, but a wiser one was to hold one big, long, attention-grabbing race per year. Five hundred miles was chosen as the distance, because that was how far a race car could go in six hours, and six hours was considered the attention-span limit of a race crowd. The entry fee for racers was set at five hundred dollars to ensure a high-quality field, and the prize money was a staggering (for 1911) twenty-five thousand dollars. Forty cars competed, eighty thousand people packed the stands on Memorial Day, and Ray Harroun, in a yellow Marmon with a pointed rear end that earned it the nickname "Wasp," finished first, at the then-lightning average speed of seventy-five miles per hour. Long, grueling, fast, rich, and (usually) exciting, the reputation of the Indianapolis 500 was established with its first race.

The 1912 race enhanced the Indy 500's fame. Ralph DePalma led the race in his Mercedes from the third lap to the 196th (out of two hundred.) He had a three-and-a-half-lap lead on local favorite Joe Dawson when his race car broke down on the back straight. Despite the fact that he now had no hope of winning, DePalma and his riding mechanic (riding mechanics were the rule at the time), Rupert Jeffkins, pushed their one-ton racer the mile and a quarter back to the pits to complete their 197th lap. Dawson in his National won, but DePalma has epitomized the competitive fire the Indy 500 inspires in racers ever since.

By 1913 there were many European carmakers and racers competing, which added even more excitement ranging from faster-revving engines to drivers who sipped champagne during pit stops. The outbreak of World War I ended the entry of foreign cars and drivers, and in 1917 and 1918 the running of the race itself.

Racing resumed in 1919, and though some foreign cars and drivers ran the Indy 500 from time to time, domestic cars and drivers came to the fore. The first "golden age" of American racing—the Miller/Duesenberg era—was about to begin.

Get Lower, Get Faster

The 1920s are considered one of the golden ages of American open wheel racing. The speedy little racers built by engineer Fred Duesenberg—the first cars with a supercharged, eight-cylinder engine—and the sleek, front-wheel-drive Miller racers, dominated the speedway—and the rest of American racing—throughout the decade.

Racing pioneers Barney Oldfield (in driver's seat) and Harry Miller pose with the FWD Special, a four-wheel-drive race car designed by Miller.

Up until World War I race-car builders had focused chiefly on straight-line speed. Their goal was horsepower, and they got it from huge, four-cylinder engines. These mammoth engines sat under high front hoods, perched on top of tall, thin tires. Because of this top-heavy design, early race cars were prone to tipping, with usually disastrous results for the driver and riding mechanic in those days before seat belts. The driver had to back off the throttle in a turn to keep the car stable.

The process of downshifting and braking before a turn, then upshifting to high gear for the straightaways, greatly reduced the average lap speed. While the thirty-three-hundred-foot-long front and back straights at Indianapolis allowed the drivers plenty of space to get back up to top speed, on smaller tracks the drivers spent all their time preparing for, and recovering from, the turns. In an effort to improve both speed and safety, the American Automobile Association (AAA), which had set the rules and prizes in racing since 1909, decided in 1920 that the new, higher-revving engines would be limited to 183 cubic inches. This led to a complete redesign, not only of the engines but of the race cars themselves.

The key to a better-handling car that did not have to be drastically slowed down in turns was a lower center of gravity. A California engineer named Harry Miller decided the way to do that was to relocate the transmission in the race car and drive the front wheels instead of the back. This eliminated the hump under the cockpit and allowed the car to take the low-slung shape still associated with racers. Miller's radical change was vindicated when his Miller Junior, driven by Bennett Hill, came back from being two laps behind the leading Duesenberg of Pete DePaolo to finish second in the 1925 race. Hill flew through the corners and pushed DePaolo to an average speed of 101.13 miles per hour, the first time the one-hundred-miles-per-hour barrier had been broken.

"For ten thrilling years, two great automotive engineers had set up a form of rivalry unmatched in skill and ingenuity," wrote legendary motor-sports journalist Brock Yates in his book about the Indianapolis 500. "The machines they gave to the sport reached speeds that remain impressive today [Yates was writing in 1961 when the average speed had reached only 139 miles per hour]. And certainly at no time in racing history has the competition been any keener. Miller's cars won five times [between 1922 and 1929], took second place five times and third place

twice. Duesenberg's record was less impressive but still admirable. His car captured three wins, took second place twice and third place three times. Ironically, Harry Miller's 1922 winning engine was carried on a chassis designed and built by Duesenberg."[2]

The golden age ended with a crash—not on the track, but on Wall Street. The Great Depression of the 1930s led to the creation of the so-called "junk formula," which attempted to cut costs by requiring the use of mostly stock (factory made and mass-produced) chassis and engine components. This change drove Harry Miller into bankruptcy, though his engines and race cars from the 1920s continued to dominate open wheel racing.

Lack of money during the depression forced other changes in racing rules. Limits were placed on the amount of oil (six gallons, with no additions during the race) and gasoline (fifteen gallons) the cars could carry. These economic measures had a payoff in safety as well, although smaller fuel tanks greatly increased the number of pit stops. Though the fuel and oil limits were temporary, some lasting safety innovations were made at that time. Crash helmets became standard gear, and in 1935 six sets of traffic lights were installed around the track. For the first time the drivers were able to learn about the race status (e.g., a yellow light signals caution due to an accident) from something other than the flags waved by the starter.

Back Home to Race in Indiana

The 1941 Indy 500, the last held before the United States entered World War II, was almost canceled by a morning fire in the garages that destroyed three cars. Before the wrecked areas could be rebuilt, the track was abandoned during the war and deteriorated rapidly. Indianapolis native Wilbur Shaw, who had won the 1937, 1939, and 1940 races, persuaded Terre Haute, Indiana, businessman Tony Hulman to buy the track for seventy thousand dollars. The purchase was concluded in November, a furious rebuilding commenced, and the Indy 500 resumed on Memorial Day 1946. Though nearly all the cars that ran dated from the late 1930s, the race drew more than one hundred thousand fans.

Shaw and Hulman saw that the newly restored interest Americans had in auto racing could either enhance the Indy 500's reputation or destroy the race entirely if the fans turned more attention to the plethora of stock-car and sprint-car races that were being held all over the country. Shaw and Hulman set out to create "the greatest spectacle in racing." Prize money was boosted to more than a quarter of a million dollars, and car specifications were modified slightly to attract the drivers and cars that were racing on the nation's smaller tracks. What happened next was nothing Shaw and Hulman could have expected.

"In the late 40s, midget racing had taken the nation by storm, and hundreds of new drivers were learning the ropes in these tiny, high-performance machines. [Midgets are front-engine racers with a wheel base less than six feet and weigh about seven hundred pounds. They race

"LADIES AND GENTLEMEN... START YOUR ENGINES!"

In 1977 Speedway matriarch Mary Hulman was forced to change the traditional call to race ("Gentlemen. . . . Start Your Engines!"), because Janet Guthrie, the first woman to qualify for the Indianapolis 500, sat in car number 27. Guthrie was beset by mechanical problems and finished twenty-seventh that year, but came back the following year to finish ninth. Lynn St. James arrived at the Brickyard in 1992, becoming the oldest rookie and Rookie of the Year at the age of forty-five. She finished eleventh. St. James ran the 1993–1995 races, but as a regular CART competitor she was closed out of the Indy 500 until 2000.

That year she and Sarah Fisher made history as the first two women to compete against each other at the Brickyard; they crashed together on the sixty-fourth lap. Fisher has gone on to post several records in IRL competition, including being the first woman to win the pole position in a race and the first to finish a race in the top three.

The introduction of the Lotus Ford in 1963, with its sleek shape and V8 engine in the rear, marked the beginning of the era of rear-engined race cars.

on quarter- to half-mile tracks.] The driving style used on the tight, paved, midget tracks demanded phenomenal reflexes and judgment that worked in inches rather than feet," says Yates. "When these men began to arrive at the Speedway in 1949 and 1950, they saw it as nothing more than an enlarged midget track and set about driving on it with the same techniques they used on smaller ovals.

"Their Indy cars were nothing more than enlarged midgets. They carried the same four-wheel torsion-bar suspensions and were fabricated with similar tubular steel frames. With these cars, the rash new group of drivers were revolutionizing Speedway racing, Suddenly, the front-wheel-drive machines, which required a special driving style completely different from anthing employed in a midget, began to look very old fashioned."[3]

The new-style cars and drivers quickly dominated the Brickyard. In 1951 Lee Wallard set a new average-speed record of

126.244 miles per hour, the first big jump in speed since 1938. He won in the same light, tough, fast car that he raced on bumpy dirt tracks and small paved ovals; the old-style cars in the field fell apart trying to keep up.

By 1954 improvements in Firestone's racing tires, which allowed for higher cornering speeds, and the introduction of fuel injectors, pushed the average speed above 130 miles per hour. By 1956 the dirt-track-style cars ruled, virtually all of them powered by Offenhauser engines that had dominated Indy since the 1930s. This "roadster" design, with the engine up front under a long, flat hood, went unaltered and unchallenged until 1963. That year Colin Chapman, an English engineer who owned the high-performance car-builder Lotus, brought to the Brickyard his revolutionary racer with the Ford V8 engine in the back. The next great era of open wheel racing was about to begin.

AFRICAN AMERICANS IN RACING

In 1991 Willy T. Ribbs, an accomplished sports car racer, became the first African American to qualify for the Indianapolis 500. Though he was a pioneer, Ribbs was far from the first black American race car driver.

During the 1920s the city of Indianapolis had a flourishing black enclave. One of its leaders, a building contractor named William Rucker, was an avid race fan; however, his ambition to get black drivers and mechanics into the big race was blocked by the segregation laws of the day. So Rucker organized the city's top black business leaders and several white car racing promoters (that included Carl Fisher of the Speedway) into the Colored Speedway Association. On August 2, 1924, the group staged the first auto race open to black drivers, an event a local newspaper dubbed "The Gold and Glory Sweepstakes."

The winner, Malcolm Hannon, set a new national record for a one-mile dirt track with an average speed of 63.5 miles per hour. But the real star of the series became Charlie Wiggins, a diminutive mechanical genius who also concocted his own racing fuel. Wiggins, who won the 1926, 1931, and 1932 races and placed second in 1929, became a local hero in Indianapolis where he ran a garage. The success of the Gold and Glory prompted other race organizers as far away as Fort Worth, Texas; Atlanta, Georgia; Chicago, Illinois; and Langhorn, Pennsylvania to stage "colored classics," according to an article by Todd Gould published in the *Indianapolis Recorder* July 2, 1927. Wiggins gained fame not only as a driver but as a car owner, mechanic, and tutor of racers. One of his white protégés, "Wild Bill" Cummings, won the Indy 500 in 1934.

The Gold and Glory Sweepstakes continued until 1936. That year a thirteen-car wreck ended both Wiggins's driving career (he lost a leg in the crash) and the race itself. The Colored Speedway Association, like most other racing groups, fell victim to the Great Depression, and the golden age of black racing came to an end.

The Age of Aerodynamics

Chapman was the first car builder to extensively use the principles of aerodynamics to design a race car. He reasoned that a car closer to the ground would create less air resistance. Moving the engine to behind the driver eliminated the need for a driveshaft running to the back wheels and thus let his racers hug the ground. Chapman pioneered the monocoque, or "tub," design of chassis construction. This meant the driver was surrounded by a solid metal structure to which the engine was bolted from behind. This not only made the car lighter and more agile, but it eventually led to major breakthroughs in driver protection.

In 1963 Chapman's Lotus, driven by the great Scots racer Jim Clark, finished a close second to the Offenhauser roadster of Parnelli Jones. The results caught the attention of American race-car builders, and the following year twelve cars were rear engined; in one of them 1959 Indy 500 winner Rodger Ward finished second.

In 1965 the spidery little cars' domination was complete. Ford-powered Lotuses registered the fastest qualifying times, which placed them in front at the start of the race. Clark won the race, one minute and fifty-nine seconds ahead of second place Jones, in a traditional roadster that ran out of fuel as he crossed the finish line. Mario Andretti, in another rear-engine car, was a close third and was named Rookie of the Year. At an average speed of 151.388 miles per hour, Clark was the first to break the 150-miles-per-hour barrier. Racing's own version of the British Invasion of the 1960s brought to America British F1 racer Graham Hill, who won the 1966 Indy 500 in his first appearance. Ironically, Hill did not win Rookie of the Year—that honor went to future world champion Jackie Stewart of Scotland, who finished third behind Jim Clark.

The 1970s and 1980s saw the domination of the turbocharged Ford-Cosworth V8 engine, which was introduced to racing by Chapman. Qualifying speeds (which determine a racer's starting position) took a quantum leap from 170 miles per hour in 1970 to 195 miles per hour only two years later, then ratcheted upward: 202 miles per hour in 1978, 224 miles per hour in 1988, and 231 miles per hour in 1995. The 1970s were dominated by the American Unser brothers—Al Unser Sr. won back-to-back races in 1970 and 1971 and again in 1978. His brother Bobby won his second Indy 500 in 1975 (his first was 1968). Johnny Rutherford, another American, also won twice in the decade.

By the mid-1980s, nearly all Indy cars were one of two models: either the March 85C or the Lola T900-Cosworth (ironically, both fully built in Britain.) This made racing extremely competitive, both at Indianapolis and on the rest of the open wheel circuits. "The championship developed into a fascinating battle of drivers," says racing journalist Gordon Kirby, "which was comparatively uncomplicated by variables in chassis, engines and tires."[4] Such parity came about partly due to market forces (two clearly superior car/engine packages that were available to any team able to afford them) and rules about tires, fuel, and engines that kept any one team or manufacturer from becoming too dominant.

These rules were set by a new sanctioning body called Championship Auto Racing Teams, or CART. CART was founded in 1978 by a group of Indy car-team owners who wanted a bigger voice in the control of their sport than the U.S. Auto Club (USAC) would allow. CART established itself as the top American open wheel racing series by the early 1980s. It assumed control of all the former USAC races, except the Indianapolis 500, and expanded into races held on road courses and city streets.

CART was very successful for about fifteen years, but economic forces, lack of leadership, and America's fundamen-

Mario Andretti was named Rookie of the Year after his third-place finish in the 1965 Indy 500.

tal dedication to oval racing began chipping away its prestige in the late 1990s. Kirby wrote as early as 1985 that bitterness was rising among smaller teams about the control the larger teams such as Penske, Patrick, Newman-Haas, and Galles had over the decision-making

LEGENDARY TRACKS—THE MILWAUKEE MILE

The Milwaukee Mile is the world's oldest existing motor racing track. Part of the Wisconsin State Fairgrounds, the track has hosted every kind of motor sports event—endurance races, motorcycles, sprint cars, stock cars, and NASCAR trucks. It was even a football field—during the 1930s the Green Bay Packers played two "home" games a year on the infield, and the 1939 NFL Championship Game (Packers 27, New York Giants 0) was played there. But its history as an open wheel racetrack is unmatched.

Barney Oldfield cracked the seventy-miles-per-hour record on the Mile in 1910, and Rex Mays broke the ninety miles-per-hour barrier in 1934. By then one-hundred-mile champ car races were an annual event; in 1948 the race was lengthened to two hundred miles.

For its first fifty-one years the Mile was a dirt track because the auto racers shared the track with horse races. Paved in 1954 it hosted two races a season—the Rex Mays Classic one hundred-miler, which became "the first race after Indy," and the Tony Bettanhausen 200 in August. In 1980 the Milwaukee Mile hosted the first CART race.

The Mile has been a happy place for legendary racing families such as the Unsers and the Andrettis. The Unsers have won nine times there, and the Andrettis have six victories. An event unique in all of motor sports occurred there in 1991 when Michael Andretti won, his cousin John finished second, and his father Mario took third—the only time members of one family have finished 1-2-3.

For its one hundredth birthday the Mile had a complete facelift, and new grandstands seat forty-five thousand fans. The centennial race on May 31, 2003, was a first—held under 1.3 million watts of light; it was Champ Car's (as CART is now known) first night race, and veteran driver Michel Jourdain's first win. Spruced up and with a full schedule, the Mile is set to go another century.

Mexico's Michel Jourdain races to victory on the famous Milwaukee Mile in May 2003.

process in the league. Discontent about the decision making and money sharing in CART eventually led to a split in 1996, with several teams jumping to the newly formed Indy Racing League (IRL) formed by Indianapolis Motor Speedway owner Tony George. At first the IRL's future looked shaky, but having sole proprietorship of the world's biggest race at the world's most famous track—coupled with some savvy business moves and a program and rules aimed at making rac-ing more accessible for smaller teams—got the upstart league on track by 2000.

Eventually it was the prestige of the Indianapolis 500 that forced several premier CART teams, including Penske, Ganassi, and Green, to move to the IRL. Their sponsors demanded the exposure that can only be had from the Memorial Day classic. While drivers, teams, and the cars attract the attention of the dedicated race fan, the Speedway itself has proven to be the top attraction in open wheel racing.

CHAPTER 2

Stock Car Racing: The South's Biggest Export

Stock car racing is the most popular kind of racing in the United States. Under the banner of the National Association for Stock Car Auto Racing (NASCAR), there are thirty-six races a season—the first in Daytona Beach, Florida, in February and the last in Atlanta, Georgia, in November. The average attendance at all but the smallest tracks is 150,000. Millions more fans watch each race on television; NASCAR's television ratings are second only to those of the National Football League (NFL). Stock car racing is not only big-time sports—it is big business.

Out of the Hills

Stock car racing's origin is the stuff of legends. The major factor in the birth of

the sport was not a love of cars, a fascination with all things mechanical, or a lust for speed, as it was in other realms of motor racing. It was the fact that alcohol was still illegal in many parts of the South, even after the repeal of Prohibition. As a result an enormous illegal liquor business sprang up, with the bulk of this liquor—or moonshine—being brewed in thousands of backwoods stills in the hills of the South then taken to the cities for distribution and sale. Transportation for that distribution network was made up of hopped-up Ford coupes with V8 "flathead" engines, driven by daring, desperate men whose livelihoods, freedom, and sometimes lives, depended on outrunning the "revenooers"—the federal agents charged with stopping the illicit trade in moonshine.

During the 1930s the moonshine runners sometimes got together to race each other, either on remote country roads or around a field. Even before World War II, the hard, flat sands of Daytona Beach, Florida, were a destination for racers and fans, a fact not lost on a local gas station owner named William Henry Getty France.

Daytona was a prime location for motor sports beginning as early as 1902. British racer Sir Malcolm Campbell went there each year during the early 1930s to attempt a new land speed record on the five-hundred-yard-wide, twenty-five-mile-long beach. However, after 1936 Campbell turned his attention to the bigger, flatter, drier Bonneville Salt Flats in Utah as a more promising place for his quest.

British racer Sir Malcolm Campbell poses with his famous "Bluebird" before attempting to break the land speed record at Daytona Beach in 1933.

Without Campbell, Daytona needed a new attraction. France, a natural-born organizer, was asked to set up a race to celebrate that year's Fourth of July and keep the race fans, and their money, coming to Daytona.

The races France staged in 1938 and 1939 were huge successes, both for the drivers and spectators. At last the moonshine runners had a place to race that was legal, organized, and run under a small but tightly enforced set of rules. For the drivers there were all kinds of prizes France had wheedled out of local merchants: rum, clothes, beer, cigars, motor oil, and credit at a used-car lot. When the fans arrived in 1939, there were grandstands, a scoreboard, and loudspeakers. France paid for almost none of it—he traded the goods for permission for the merchants to put up advertising signs. Clearly Bill France knew how to run a race.

The Birth of NASCAR

There is little doubt that "Big Bill" France would have moved ahead quickly but for the intervention of World War II. After the war France decided to resume his stock car race promotions, but the AAA, the

---

RACING DYNASTIES: THE PETTY FAMILY

No family is more closely identified with any sport than the Pettys are with stock car racing. No other sport has ever seen four generations from the same family reach the highest level, though the Pettys time in that unique status was tragically short.

Lee Petty (1915–2000) took the family Buick to Charlotte, North Carolina, and drove it in the first NASCAR race there in 1948. By the time he retired in 1964, he had won the first Daytona 500, fifty-four other races, and three Grand National titles.

His son, Richard, born in 1937, was the greatest stock car driver in history. "King" Richard won two hundred races and seven national titles. Whether he drove a Plymouth, a Dodge, or a Chevy, the younger Petty always wore the number 43, and he made STP a household name all over the country, not just in the South. Unlike most of his contemporaries and stock car racers of today, Richard Petty was equally at home on road courses as he was on ovals. The thirty-four-year span of his career (1958–1992), as well as his brand of complete dominance of his sport, might never be equaled.

Richard's son, Kyle, born in 1961, began his NASCAR career at age twenty. In more than twenty seasons he has won only eight races; during his career he has tried his hand at several other interests, such as motorcycles, acting, and singing.

Kyle's son, Adam, born in 1981, showed great promise in the Busch series, the step below the Winston Cup, and moved up to the big show in April 2000. But on May 12, 2000, less than five weeks after his great-grandfather, Lee, died, the youngest Petty hit the wall at the New Hampshire Speedway while practicing for a Busch race. He died instantly, and with him, perhaps, so did the Petty dynasty.

---

only national racing sanctioning body in the United States at the time, was not interested in what it considered a passing fad. France realized that the way to stimulate interest was to have a championship, so he organized the National Championship Stock Car Circuit (NCSCC) in 1946.

France ran his races at several dirt ovals in the Carolinas and Georgia. However, he was troubled by the fact that each track owner tried to set his own rules of racing, and some owners were less than scrupulous about things like gate receipts and prize money. In February 1948 France gathered southern racing's most influential men and proposed a central body to sanction races.

As business analyst and historian Robert Hagstrom writes, "He began by describing his vision: a central body whose sole purpose would be 'to unite all stock car racing under one set of rules . . . set up a benevolent fund and a national point standings whereby only one stock car driver would be crowned National Champion.' The rules, he declared, would be consistent, enforceable, and ironclad. The regulations would be designed to ensure close competition, for they all knew that close side-by-side racing was what the fans cheered for. Finally, he argued, the organizing body should promote a racing division dedicated solely to standard street stock cars, the same cars that could be bought at automobile dealerships. Fans would love these races, France argued, because they could identify with the cars."[5]

Though everyone present was invited to invest, only four people did—one of them was Bill France. This set the stage for the France family's ongoing control of NASCAR. NASCAR was officially incorporated on February 15, 1948—the day France made one of the best decisions in the history of U.S. business.

The Biggest Sports Event in the South

Harold Brasington, a heavy-equipment owner in Darlington, South Carolina, made another great decision. A race fan, Brasington came home from his first visit to Indianapolis in 1949 with a vision of a big track for stock cars to run on. Met with skepticism from everyone except Bill France, he started building his 1.25-mile speedway just outside town, all by himself. What everyone in Darlingon thought was "Brasington's folly" turned out to be one of racing's great success stories.

Qualification for the first Southern 500, in August 1950, took fifteen days because seventy-five cars entered. On the morning of the race, Labor Day, the nine thousand grandstand seats filled immediately, and Brasington started letting people into the infield. The fans were treated to an interesting race with a new twist—racing on

As a pit crew works feverishly to get a car back on the track, a capacity crowd watches the action at the Southern 500 at Darlington Raceway.

asphalt. Most of the drivers ran their cars the same way they did on dirt tracks—flat out. The hard surface chewed up the tires, and in those days before hydraulic jacks and air guns, a tire change took minutes, not seconds. But a savvy Plymouth driver named Johnny Mantz held a steady seventy-six miles per hour and finished the race first, on the same tires he started on. Slow and steady had won the race, but Darlington was off to a fast start.

The next year's Southern 500 was won by ex-moonshine runner Fonty Flok, who jumped on the hood of his Oldsmobile in his standard race uniform—Bermuda shorts—and led the assembled thirty-five thousand fans in singing "Dixie." By 1955 the race was the biggest sporting event in the South, and it has sold out all seventy-five thousand tickets available for each of the two races a season every year since then.

The Superspeedways Arrive

Surprisingly, Brasington's success at Darlington did not convince the skeptics that the future of stock car racing lay anywhere but on its traditional little dirt ovals. But France knew better. The 1960s became the decade of the superspeedways.

France started first on his home turf, Daytona. He gave the shrine of American speed a fitting temple—a 2.5-mile tri-oval, with huge, sweeping turns banked at thirty-one degrees. The size and speed of the track awed even veteran racers like Lee Petty. "I'll tell you what, there wasn't a man there who wasn't scared of that place. We never had raced on a track like that before."[6] Petty was not too intimidated to win the inaugural race, though, in 1959.

More than two hundred thousand fans flocked to the first Speed Week, which switched from the beach to the track that February. Instant success convinced France that he was correct about the appeal of big tracks, and the following year construction began on three new superspeedways—Atlanta, Georgia; Charlotte, North Carolina; and Hanford, California. Finally, in 1969,

---

LEGENDARY TRACKS: DAYTONA

Daytona, Florida, was a legendary racing place long before there was a permanent track there. Racers hit the flat, wide beaches in the early twentieth century; there were several attempts made there to break the land speed record in the 1930s. Stock car racing arrived in the late 1930s with a track that incorporated the beach and the road parallel to it. However, motorcycle racing actually drew more participants and spectators during the years just before and after World War II. For a time there were two sand/road ovals, a 2.2-miler for cars and a 4.2-miler for motorcycles. By the 1950s Bill France had the auto race well organized and sanctioned under his NASCAR organization, and the racing was fast and furious. But the problems of driving on the beach, chiefly blowing sand and high tides that could narrow the track drastically, led him to build the huge oval that now epitomizes Daytona.

A 2.5-mile tri-oval, forty feet wide and with three three-thousand-foot-long, thirty-one degrees turns, Daytona was like no other track in the world when it opened in 1959. At this, the "spiritual home" of NASCAR, the stock-car season kicks off with the Speed Weeks in February, two weeks of all kinds of NASCAR racing that culminates in the Daytona 500. Nearly half a million dedicated fans spend their winter vacation at Speed Weeks, and an equal number brave the summer heat for the Firecracker 400 on the Fourth of July.

Daytona is also the site of another legendary race, the 24 Hours of Daytona, held in January on a 3.5-mile course that incorporates the tri-oval with a winding, infield road course. The 24 Hours, run since 1966, is a grueling, four-thousand-plus-mile endurance race, the only one of its kind in the United States. Daytona is the second-most prestigious race in this series, outranked only by the venerable 24 Hours of Le Mans.

France took a crossroads in the middle of nowhere, Alabama, and turned it into one of the most electrifying names in racing—Talladega. Talladega is wide enough for three cars to run abreast and is longer than Daytona by 0.16 mile. It is common for racing speeds to reach two hundred miles per hour, though the use of restrictor plates on this track and Daytona are supposed to limit the speeds somewhat.

With the addition of the big tracks, each of which was guaranteed two races per year, many of the old-style traditional dirt tracks lost out. This trend accelerated when tobacco company R.J. Reynolds signed on as the principle sponsor in 1971. Looking for a bigger bang for its sponsorship buck, Reynolds pressed NASCAR to shorten the season from forty-six races to thirty-one and to concentrate on the tracks that attracted larger crowds. By 1972 there were only nine short tracks still on the schedule—places such as Hickory Speedway, Columbia Speedway, and Greenville-Pickens fell to hosting only local racing. Even the small tracks that remained on the schedule—the one-milers Dover, Bristol, Phoenix, and New Hampshire—all hold upwards of one hundred thousand people. The two smallest tracks are both in Virginia—half-mile Martinsville and three-quarter-mile Richmond—have also increased their seating to more than eighty thousand. In NASCAR those kinds of numbers matter as much as the numbers on the track. They affirm that stock car racing is a show many people want to watch.

Old Engines in New Cars

In all the years since NASCAR has sanctioned races, it has never lost sight of the idea that what it is selling is a show. To speed, durability, and safety in the race car, stock car racing has added another vital racing element: entertainment. Every decision about NASCAR racing is taken with an eye to keeping it competitive, affordable for the race teams, and attractive to the average fan. One of the routes NASCAR has taken to stay on this course is to stick to traditional technology.

Though everyone associated with the series admits privately that there is not much that is "stock" on a stock car these days, NASCAR prides itself on not adopting every technological innovation that comes along. Each year it decides which American-made cars are eligible for racing, usually a Buick, Chevrolet, Ford, Mercury, Dodge, or Pontiac. (Oldsmobiles were considered before that division of General Motors closed; Japanese car makers are clamoring to be included and Toyota trucks now race in the NASCAR Craftsman truck series.) Usually the nod goes to two or three models, depending on the level of support offered by the manufacturers.

Nowhere is NASCAR's resistance to change more evident than in its racing engines. They must be standard, production-based, V8s of a design that is virtually unchanged since the 1960s. In fact, the type of engine in a stock car—cast iron, with push rods and a four-barrel carburetor—is now only available in a few kinds of truck engines. NASCAR's decision makers, however, are not embarrassed by their backwardness. "We fully realize that our engines are fairly prehistoric," director of competition John Darby told *Autoweek* in March 2003. "If you look at the engines in production cars, they are far more advanced. But we have a simple and reliable piece, and in the grand scheme of things we're pretty comfortable with what we have."[7]

Car and engine specifications have changed only slightly since the 1960s. Engine rules limit the amount of horsepower the motors can generate, which in turn controls the top speed a car can achieve. Cars must weigh at least thirty-four hundred pounds, including all fluids. Each car's weight is adjusted for that of its driver; if a driver weighs less than two hundred pounds, the car must carry extra weights, in ten pound increments, to even things out.

Brake and suspension designs date back to the 1960s as well, and the car is not linked to computers in the pits the way it is in the top levels of open wheel racing.

LIKE A SUPER BOWL, ONLY BETTER

The economic benefit to a city or region from just one major NASCAR race is nearly as great as that from hosting football's Super Bowl. The city of Charlotte, North Carolina, estimates that fans generate more than $70 million in the region during the Coca-Cola 600, which is held at the Lowe's Motor Speedway in suburban Concord. That is in one weekend, and Lowe's hosts two major races a year. Rick Horrow, a professor of sports law at Harvard University and an expert in the economics of sports, says in *The NASCAR Way* by Robert Hagstrom that that sum exceeds the potential income generated by any other major sports event in the United States—such as the National Collegiate Athletic Association Final Four—except that of the Super Bowl. "And a community with a large track gets that same impact every year, and without the risk of having a losing team, waiting its turn to have a Super Bowl, or worse, having a team owner move to another city," he says. Racing turns oil and rubber into gold.

All the on-the-spot decisions are made by the driver and/or the team manager, without much more technical data available to them than there was in the 1960s.

The reliance on the simple, tried, and true is all in the name of keeping racing relatively affordable and, equally important, equitable. NASCAR does not want to see a few rich teams spending millions of dollars to eke out a few extra tenths of a mile per hour, or the same handful of teams and drivers on the podium week after week. The tight restrictions on technology keep teams'—and the public's—attention focused on the drivers and the overall performance of the car. The idea is that, on any given race day, any race team could reasonably hope to win. In fact, driver daring and pit-crew skill are often all that make the difference between winning and losing.

"At the end of the day, when someone wins a race, we still like to be able to say that the race was won by the best driver, the best crew, and the best strategy," says Darby. "We want to take as much of the other stuff out as we can."[8]

A driver willing to take risks and a highly skilled pit crew like this one can make the difference between winning and losing.

Speeding Billboards

This is not to say that racing smarts and a heavy right foot are all that are needed to win a stock car race. It also takes money.

Nowadays sponsorship in sports, both amateur and professional, is taken for granted. In fact, it has been around in auto racing since the very first races. Commercial interests, some of which have no connection whatsoever to cars, have put up money in return for display-ing their name and/or wares to the race goers. But NASCAR is widely regarded as the sports entity that brought sponsorship to its present status. The thirty-one-season association between NASCAR and Winston cigarettes, which ended with the 2003 season, is more than a textbook example—it is the model for the most successful sports sponsorship pacts today.

In 1970 Congress passed a law that banned cigarette commercials on television. The same year both Ford and Chrysler announced that they were withdrawing factory support from stock car racing teams, in effect ending the free supply of engines and chassis. Racer and team owner Junior Johnson, whose hillbilly moonshiner image (and real life past) camouflaged a sharp, creative mind, realized that the cigarette companies would be looking for a new place to put the millions of dollars they had previously spent on television. He approached R.J. Reynolds, based near his home in North Carolina, and brokered a meeting between CEO Ralph Seagreaves and NASCAR president Bill France. In 1971 R.J. Reynolds sponsored two races under the Winston banner and was pleased with the results. The tobacco giant found that NASCAR fans were extremely loyal and that motor sports offered a huge, untapped marketing opportunity. For what is now the paltry fee of one hundred thousand dollars, the NASCAR Grand National Championship trophy became the Winston Cup, and Winston and stock cars became indelibly linked.

There is a difference between advertising and sponsorship, says sports business expert Robert Hagstrom. "Advertising is a direct and overt message to consumers. If successful, it generates a near-term purchase. Sponsorship, on the other hand, generates a more subtle message that, if successful, creates a lasting bond between consumers and the company."[9] For better or worse R.J. Reynolds and other cigarette makers forged a bond with stock car fans based on the perceived "outlaw" status of both the sport and the product. Soon racetrack crowds were proudly wearing T-shirts and caps with cigarette logos that the tobacco companies handed out for free. The fans were happy—they had a "uniform" and a way of identifying themselves and their race-fan brethren. The tobacco companies were very happy—they were spending money pitching their product to a neatly targeted audience that had shown itself to be very receptive, rather than an indifferent (and increasingly hostile) mass audience.

The success of this partnership made other corporations take notice. Budweiser, Tide, Kellogg's, Crisco (a staple of southern cookery), Coors, and Maxwell House soon signed up to sponsor cars and teams and found themselves reaping the benefits of fan loyalty. Seventy of the Fortune 500 corporations, many with no apparent connection to motor sports, have significant stakes in NASCAR racing, says Hagstrom. Clearly, the "win on Sunday, sell on Monday" principle applies to more than just car sales.

Sponsorship involves more than putting up a banner or slapping a logo on the side of a car. NASCAR's sponsors are invited to become part of, and even to help create, the stock car racing community. The presence of a sponsor's name or logo on a car or uniform identifies that company as part of the community. In addition, the high emotion of the race promotes the fans' identification with the sponsors, Hagstrom believes.

The ultimate in sponsorship is sponsoring a NASCAR team. For $1.5 million a year for a back-marker car, or $10 million a year for a championship winner, a team sponsor gets to cover a car, its driver, pit crew, equipment, and the tractor trailer that carries it all, with its name and logo. Sponsor names become linked to the driver and team—Jeff Gordon's car is the DuPont; Terry Labonte's is the Kellogg's. The fact that major sponsorship changes are extremely rare shows that the companies that put their millions into stock car racing are satisfied with the results.

NASCAR's high value was clearly demonstrated when Winston announced in the winter of 2003 that falling profits dictated their withdrawal from sponsoring the series. It took only four months for a new sponsor—cell phone giant Nextel—to come on board for ten years, reportedly for $750 million, though the entire sponsorship package may actually be worth $1 billion. Winston was in-

Terry Labonte's racing suit displays the logos of the various companies that sponsor his team.

vesting approximately $30–60 million a year in NASCAR; Nextel's stake will be at least $75 million annually. *AutoWeek* reported that "Nextel plans to aggressively promote its connection to the racing series, which should raise NASCAR's profile in the national media even higher."[10]

Everyone associated with racing—drivers, teams, and fans—recognizes the importance of sponsorship to the very existence of their sport. This creates an unusually high degree of loyalty from NASCAR and its fans to the sponsors.

NASCAR's decision makers have made it fairly easy for interested companies to put money into sponsoring cars, teams, events, and even website pages and single-shot prizes. They encourage companies to tie their sponsorship to other marketing activities such as product promotions, corporate entertaining, and in-house morale building. In this way the sponsors' employees, vendors, and customers are drawn into the stock car family. And they, too, become part of the show.

CHAPTER 3

Formula One: The World Series of Racing

Formula One (F1), or Grand Prix, racing represents the pinnacle of technology and achievement in auto racing on the global stage. Race-car manufacturers and sponsors invest tens of millions of dollars in the chase for the Formula One World Championship every year. This flood of money allows race teams to grasp every possible advantage on the racetrack, no matter how small or expensive. This has led critics to charge that technological advancement is more important than actual racing in F1, and has allowed only the most financially well-endowed teams to be consistently competitive. However, this has not diminished F1's glamour or appeal to audiences all around the world.

Formula One is the most international of all racing series, with events on every continent except Africa and Antarctica. Still, the series continues to reflect its European roots in many ways—the dominant teams bear names of legendary European car builders such as Ferrari, Renault, BMW, and Mercedes, and all its race venues are either temporary street circuits or purpose-built road courses, many of which incorporate public roads.

When racing began in the late nineteenth century, Europe, relatively compact and densely populated compared to North America, had an extensive road system. To this day Grand Prix are always run on courses that are either similar to regular roads or are actually temporarily set up on public roads and even, in the case of Monaco, city streets. The one exception is the U.S. Grand Prix, where the cars race part of each lap on the legendary oval of Indianapolis before turning onto the infield road course.

The Birth of the Grand Prix

Historians consider the Gordon Bennett Trophy, a race from Paris to Rouen in France first held on June 14, 1900, as the first international car race. It was the brain-child of James Gordon Bennett, flamboyant publisher of the *New York Herald*, who had a genius for putting his money where it would reap the most publicity for his newspapers. The Gordon Bennett race was also the first to set a "formula," a set of specifications that all the competing cars had to meet, though the Gordon Bennett Trophy formula only limited the weight of the cars. (Modern formulas set precise measures for things such as engine size, the number of cylinders

Formula One, or Grand Prix, racing is the most international form of car racing, with events held on virtually every continent.

FAMILY DYNASTIES: THE ASCARIS AND THE HILLS

Alberto Ascari was only seven years old when his father, Antonio, was killed leading the 1925 French Grand Prix. That did not deter him from becoming the first Grand Prix driver to follow his fa-

Alberto Ascari (right) at the Grand Prix of Modena in 1950.

ther's career path. The junior Ascari (born in 1918) became one of the stars of Ferrari, winning thirty-three Formula One races and back-to-back World Championships in 1952 and 1953. In a chilling coincidence Alberto was killed testing a Ferrari at Monza, thirty years to the day that his father died.

Damon Hill, who won the World Championship in 1996, was fifteen when his father—two-time champion and Indy 500 winner Graham Hill—died in a plane crash in 1975. Though he had little memory of his father's glory years in racing, the young Hill also had the "speed genes." Despite arriving in Formula One at the advanced age of thirty-two, Hill had four successful seasons and a championship for the Williams racing team. Nevertheless, Hill's contract with the team was not renewed, and he ended his career after two seasons in uncompetitive cars.

an engine can have, the size and configuration of the car, etc.) Each national automobile association could enter three cars, and the winner's home country would host the next race. French drivers and cars won the first two races. Then, in 1903, British driver Selwyn Edge won the race, from Paris, France, to Innsbruck, Austria, with an average speed of thirty-two miles per hour.

Edge's win not only brought the event to Britain (actually, the race was run on a makeshift road course in Ireland) but ignited British interest in auto racing for

the first time. That race was won by a German team, which took the 1904 event to the Taunus Forest outside Hamburg, Germany—a seventy-nine-mile-long course. Frenchman Leon Thery won the four-lap event, which brought the 1905—and final—Gordon Bennett Trophy race back to France. Thery won again, largely thanks to being able to practice in advance on the course at Clermont-Ferrand (later the venue for many runnings of the French Grand Prix).

The Gordon Bennett Trophy races fell victim to the desire of many auto builders to have races that were better organized and held on dedicated race circuits. Car sales were booming on both sides of the Atlantic, and manufacturers were acutely aware of the two-fold benefits of going racing: testing technological advances and getting publicity.

The car builders agreed to hand the administration of races and rule making over to the Automobile Club of France. The first Grand Prix, run on June 26 and 27, 1906, was set out on a roughly triangular sixty-four-mile course; the race distance was 769 miles. The chief technical rule limited each cars' weight to one thousand kilograms (2,426 pounds) and fuel consumption to eight gallons per sixty-two miles. The cars' exhaust pipes were to be directed upward so the drivers behind would not be asphyxiated by fumes, and the driver and mechanic had to be aboard the car at all times. The race was run in two stages, with the cars being locked up overnight in a secure area so they could not be worked on—a precursor of today's *parc fermé* (literally, closed parking), where modern race cars are scrutinized for rule compliance.

The race was won by Hungarian Ferenc Szisz, but French honor was salvaged by his race car: a French-built Renault. However, strong showings by German, Italian, British, and even American cars and drivers proved that the rest of the world was

now taking racing as seriously as the French.

"Thus opened a new era in which the art of daring was transformed into the science of progress, drivers became full-time professionals and the first racing teams were organized," say Italian automobile historians Giuseppe Guzzardi and Enzo Rizzo. "A blend of professionalism and enthusiasm, of economic interests and passion, of risk and success, surrounded all motor racing events of the era and the sport became an instrument of political propaganda, a technological laboratory, a gravitational center of the *beau monde*, an advertising medium and a passion inaccessible to the majority."[11]

Europe Goes Racing

Racing did not remain "inaccessible" for long. In the years leading up to World War I, most of the classic European races were inaugurated: Italy's Targa Floria and Mille Miglia, France's Le Mans endurance race, and most of the national Grand Prix such as the British Grand Prix held on the world's first dedicated motor-racing track, Brooklands, in 1907. These races attracted hundreds of thousands of spectators, many of whom camped out on roadsides for days to watch the cars hurtle by in just a few seconds.

The 1914 French Grand Prix was held on the eve of World War I. It was a French-German duel, presaging the conflict that was only weeks away. The German Daimlers dominated, taking the top three places. Racing in Europe then disappeared until 1921, as war devastated both the landscape of Europe and the auto industries and decimated an entire generation of young men.

LEGENDARY TRACKS: MONACO

The "Race of 100 Corners" screams through the streets of Monte Carlo, Monaco, every May. Virtually unchanged since 1929, this extraordinarily difficult race is the most glamour-ridden event on the F1 calendar and the most coveted trophy for the drivers. Through sharp turns and hairpin curves, entirely on city streets, the race cars pass within mere feet of storefronts, houses, and the famed Casino, along Monte Carlo's glittering waterfront packed with luxurious yachts, and even through a tunnel. Accidents are common on the tight, twisting, 2.1-mile course, though there has been only one fatality (Lorenzo Bandini in 1967), and race cars flip into the water only in the movies. "Monaco separates the men from the boys," say Giuseppe Guzzardi and Enzo Rizzo in their book *The Century of Motor Racing*. "To win here, a driver needs innate talent rather than raw speed, and frequently an ability to drive in the wet given the number of times it has rained during the race." The acknowledged rain masters, Graham Hill (five wins) and Ayrton Senna (six wins) dominated Monaco during their careers.

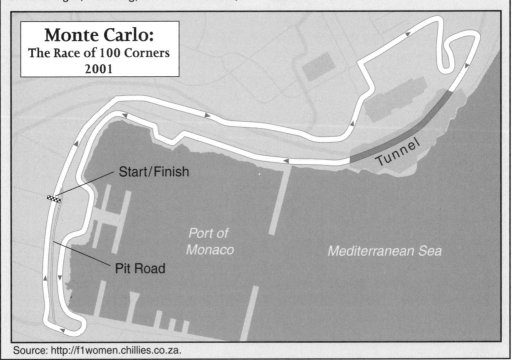

Monte Carlo:
The Race of 100 Corners
2001

Start/Finish

Pit Road

Tunnel

Port of Monaco

Mediterranean Sea

Source: http://f1women.chillies.co.za.

The war had an immediate impact on American racing as well. Grand Prix had been held in various places in the United States since 1907, including Long Island, New York; Savannah, Georgia; and California. European cars and drivers had raced at Indianapolis. With the disappearance of their overseas competitors, American car builders and the American race-going public turned all their interest to paved oval racing. Though Americans Jimmy Murphy and Ralph DePalma finished first and second in Duesenbergs at the 1921 French Grand Prix, after that trans-Atlantic competition virtually disappeared for almost forty years, except for a brief appearance by the Europeans at Indianapolis in the late 1930s. It was not until well into the "modern" era of Formula One, in 1959, that Grand Prix racing returned to the United States.

Technology Takes Off

The resurgence of European racing in the 1920s saw a huge leap in technical innovations. The Italian-made Fiats dominated the early years, with their streamlined torpedo shape, independent suspension, and supercharged eight-cylinder engines. The great track at Monza, in northern Italy, was built largely as a test facility for the automaker, and Grand Prix were held in Italy, Belgium, and Spain.

However, while the race cars were becoming ever more precision built, the rules governing the races were chaotic and irrational. In the absence of an international sanctioning body with universal regulations and the ability to enforce them, each national auto club could (and did) set rules to favor its own teams. There was also little regulation of the running of the races.

The International Association of Automobile Clubs (IAAC) attempted to step into the rules quagmire in 1926. It mandated a displacement of only 1.5 liters, which sent the engine builders scrambling to modify their machines from twelve cylinders down to eight without losing horsepower. The rules were modified later in the season to allow for two-liter displacement, but the change drove several great manufacturers out of Grand Prix racing, either because of the cost of changing their formula or as a protest against the new rules. The AIACR (to use its French initials) also required single-seat cockpits, thus eliminating the riding mechanic, and reduced the minimum weight to 1,323 pounds.

Finally, in 1931 after much acrimony, all the rules were scrapped. The only limit was on the length of the races—a minimum of five hours and a maximum of ten. Many historians and race aficionados consider the 1930s to be a golden age of racing because the absence of rules allowed for unbridled experimentation with engines and chassis. However, the German and Italian teams demonstrated the power of money, as large, government-funded budgets allowed them to pull far ahead of other teams.

By 1932 both Adolf Hitler and Benito Mussolini were in power in Germany and Italy, respectively, and they invested heavily in their nations' auto industries and racing programs as a way to prove the superiority of their political systems. Five teams dominated racing for the entire decade: Italy's Alfa Romeo, Maserati, and Bugatti, and Germany's Mercedes and, later, Auto Union. Horsepower increased rapidly, but teams also began to concentrate on building lighter cars. When the Auto Union racer debuted in 1936, its sixteen-cylinder engine delivered 520 horsepower to a car that weighed only sixteen hundred pounds. The combination boosted top speeds to over 180 miles per hour. However, the finishing order of several races is suspect, as it is known that some drivers were ordered to allow others to win certain races for political reasons.

The Modern Era Arrives

World War II ended all international racing between 1940 and 1945. As in the United States, when European competition restarted, the cars were vintage 1930s models. Even as late as 1950 and 1951, the first two Formula One. World Championships were won by Nino Farina and Juan Manuel Fangio, respectively, driving fifteen-year-old Alfa Tipo 159s that had spent the war hidden under canvas in an Italian cheese factory.

The Formula One Championships

The history of Grand Prix racing is divided into two periods: The first, from 1906 to 1950, is sometimes referred to as the "Grand Prix era." The second, and current, period is known as the "modern era." When competition resumed in Europe shortly after World War II, it was apparent that the various types of racing needed to be classified and rules set. Modern Grand Prix racing was organized as Formula One World Driving Championship under the authority of the International Automobile Federation (known as the FIA, using the initials of its name in French) in 1950.

The same year, the FIA created the Formula One Constructors' Championship for the car builders. In the fifty-two seasons until 2003, the team of the World Championship driver has lost the manufacturers' title only seven times. This can happen because a team may have more than one driver who can score points for the constructor; thus consistently high finishes by two drivers on a team can outscore the team of the championship-winning driver.

To win either the drivers' or constructors' championship, competitors must score points that are awarded for each place at

STOPPING FOR LUNCH

Racing was once a very different sport: gracious, gentlemanly, almost leisurely. At the 1925 Belgian Grand Prix, there were only seven cars from two teams entered, four French Delages and three Italian Alfa Romeos. The race should have been a superb contest between two types of race cars which were superior, but for different reasons. The Delage racers boasted supercharged one hundred eighty-horsepower engines mounted on a chassis that the French team hoped was strong enough to withstand such high speed. The Alfas, on the other hand, generated less horsepower, but chassis developments had made them better balanced and easier to drive.

When breakdowns had forced all four French cars out of the race by midpoint, the Alfa Romeo team manager called his cars into the pits and spread out a veritable banquet for his drivers and pit crews. During the unscheduled lunch break, the cars were polished and refueled. Then the drivers strolled back to their cars under a storm of catcalls and whistles from the crowd, and finished the race.

was also given a point, and the points-paying positions stretched to eighth in 2001. By 2003 the winning driver scored ten points, the runner-up eight, third place six, and so on down to one. There has not been a point awarded for fastest lap in several years.

At first the "world" designation in World Championship was a bit of an exaggeration: The races that counted towards the championship were few in number and held only in Europe. However, by the late 1950s and early 1960s, the traditional British, French, Belgian, Spanish, Monaco, and Italian Grand Prix had been joined by races in Mexico, Argentina, Brazil, and the United States. There has been a Japanese Grand Prix since 1976, a Canadian Grand Prix since 1978, and an Australian Grand Prix since 1985. Singapore and Malaysia have hosted races in the twenty-first century, and F1 returned to the United States in 2000 after nearly twenty years' absence.

Formula One in the 1950s

In the 1950s racing was still harking back to the 1930s. The tracks were mostly public roads marked off by straw bales, and the races lasted hours. The cars were still heavy and though speeds increased steadily, tire technology did not keep up. This caused many serious accidents, both in testing and racing. As in the prewar era, few drivers were exclusively employed as Formula

the finish. The points system has evolved as much as the rest of the rules of F1 racing. In the 1950s the race winner scored eight points, the second-place driver six, and the third-place driver four. The fourth and fifth places picked up three and two points, respectively, and one point was given to the racer who drove the fastest lap. After 1960 the sixth place

One competitors; most also raced in sports cars, endurance events, hill climbs, and rallies. Car builders, as well, placed their cars in many different kinds of events.

Argentina's Juan Manuel Fangio was the king of F1 in the 1950s, winning five championships between 1951 and 1957 driving for Mercedes, Maserati, and Ferrari. His record of twenty-four wins in fifty-one starts, with twenty-eight pole positions, stood until the 1980s.

As European car makers began to compete for the growing passenger car market, some dropped their racing efforts due to financial pressures. The 1950s saw the withdrawal of Alfa Romeo, Maserati, and Mercedes from Formula One racing, though the latter did so because of the tragedy at the 1955 Le Mans when one of its race cars went off the track and killed eighty-three spectators.

Evolution of the Point System

Finishing Position	1	2	3	4	5	6	7	8	Best Lap
Year	POINTS EARNED								
1950–1959	8	6	4	3	2	0	0	0	1
1960	8	6	4	3	2	1	0	0	**
1961–1990*	9	6	4	3	2	1	0	0	**
1991–2002	10	6	4	3	2	1	0	0	**
2003	10	8	6	5	4	3	2	1	**

* Only the best eleven results obtained by each driver during the season were computed toward the final points standings.

** Best Lap points not awarded.

As some of the large teams withdrew from competiton, the door opened for some innovative new teams. Though Enzo Ferrari, by then considered the dean of Formula One car builders, derisively called them *garagistes*, or teams that worked out of little garages, the new teams changed motor racing forever.

Times A-Changin'

Like every other part of society, motor racing saw seismic changes in both technology and business during the 1960s. The new, independent teams like Colin Chapman's Lotus, Dan Gurney's Eagle, and Jack Brabham's Repco, led the change to nimble, mid- and rear-engine cars. Racing engineers began to design cars that followed principles of aerodynamics and down force; speeds took a sudden jump because race cars now offered less wind resistance, and harnessing down force made them more stable and responsive to steering. For both reasons rear wings suddenly sprouted on race cars. The wings actually helped hold the now-much-faster cars on the track. Higher speeds were also due to better tires, a great leap afforded by nylon fibers and synthetic rubbers. Tires also became wider, lower in profile, and could be engineered with varying degrees of adhesion, or "stickiness." This made for better grip and allowed faster cornering.

In 1966 the engine formula changed to three liters, with a minimum car weight of eleven hundred pounds. Chapman brokered a union between American giant Ford and the tiny British company Cosworth to create a race engine that dominated both F1 and American racing until the 1980s. This combination won 155 Grand Prix while powering many different types of race cars. The Ford-Cosworth engine was the first to reliably deliver four hundred horsepower. This also began a trend that continued into the twenty-first century of the car and engine being built by separate companies; by 2003 only Ferrari built both for itself.

These advances came with an unfortunate side effect. In many cases the tracks that had been used for decades were not designed to safely handle cars running at such high speeds. As in American open wheel racing at the time, there was a rash of fatal accidents that brought the issue of safety to the fore.

The deaths of world champions Jim Clark, Jo Schlesser, Lorenzo Bandini, and nearly a dozen other drivers in the last five years of the 1960s created great concern for driver and track safety. For the first time, racers, teams, and race fans began to think that death was not necessarily an inescapable part of racing. The fact that the fearless Jackie Stewart, a three-time world champion (1969, 1971, and 1973), made safety his cause removed any suspicion of

YANKS OVER THERE

Only one American race car has won a modern Grand Prix—an Eagle driven by Dan Gurney at the Belgian Grand Prix in 1967. Nevertheless, dozens of American drivers have raced—and won—in Formula One races since the sport's beginning. Two—Phil Hill for Ferrari in 1960 and Mario Andretti for Lotus in 1978—have won the World Championship. The list of American drivers who have raced in Formula One includes some famous names, such as Gurney, Troy Ruttman, Peter Revson, Eddie Cheever, Michael Andretti, and Danny Sullivan. Not only have many Americans raced in Formula One, many former Grand Prix drivers have found successful second careers in American racing. Emerson Fittipaldi, twice the F1 champion, built an even longer and more successful second career in CART. The 1992 world champion, Nigel Mansell, won the 1993 CART championship and finished third at Indianapolis, but he chose to attempt an F1 comeback rather than build a new career in North America.

Some young veterans of American open wheel racing have moved into Formula One. Jacques Villeneuve, son of the 1970s F1 star Gilles, has had the most success. After winning the CART championship (the youngest driver to do so) in 1994 and the 1995 Indianapolis 500, Villeneuve won the World Championship for the Williams team in 1997. Two successive CART champions, Juan Montoya and Christiano da Matta, have also made the move to the international series.

Dan Gurney waves after winning a 1967 race in England.

cowardice on the part of drivers campaigning for more safety. Fireproof overalls; stronger, full-face helmets; guard rails; and the beginnings of trackside emergency medical care appeared in the late 1960s.

Those fireproof overalls started to be covered with insignia, as well, when the FIA dropped the rules prohibiting advertising on cars and drivers. Ironically, the sudden appearance of sponsor logos was due to the fact that three major sponsors/suppliers for all F1 teams—the oil companies Esso and BP and the tire manufacturer Firestone—withdrew all their support at the end of the 1967 season to save money. This meant the end of free fuel, lubricants, and tires, and threw many teams into desperate financial straits.

The sponsorship flood breached an aesthetic barrier in 1968 when the first cars painted with sponsor names and symbols appeared. To this day many race fans regret the disappearance of the traditional "national" colors, such as Lotus's British racing green. French government sponsored cars occasionally sport their country's time-honored blue, but only Ferrari still flaunts its Italian red.

More Money, More Rules

With sponsorship came money, in large quantities. It allowed the successful teams, who attracted the most sponsorship, to put more effort into engineering and technology, which then set them even further ahead of the less successful teams.

Sponsorship allowed wealthy teams to spend millions seeking even the tiniest advantage, one that could disappear in one or two races as the other teams learned about the new innovation and copied it. After only a few uses, many costly tweaks were banned as unfair by the sanctioning body, the Federation Internationale du Sport Automobile (FISA), which took control of Formula One within the FIA. Costs took another massive leap when carbon fiber, which is ultralightweight and extremely strong, began to be used to build the monocoques, or tubs, that hold the driver and form the core of the chassis and brakes.

Most of the technical focus during the 1970s was on "ground effects," or ways of keeping the cars firmly on the track even at high speed. Lotus's Chapman was the master of ground effects, and his Lotus 78 and 79 racers, with front and rear wings, carried Mario Andretti to the World Championship in 1978, making him the second American (the first was Phil Hill in 1961) to win the title. Other teams scrambled to keep up, experimenting with side skirts, vacuum turbines, and even—briefly—six wheels.

The next step in technology was actually a backward one in a sense. In 1979 Renault reintroduced the turbocharged engine, which had been successful for Alfa Romeo in the 1950s. While some teams, notably Ferrari, tried to stay competitive with conventional engines and ground effects, by the early 1980s it was apparent that turbocharged engines were far more powerful. However, the cost of developing them, as well as the other high-tech chassis innovations and the evolution of racing fuel to something closer to jet fuel than gasoline, drove many teams out of the sport.

Perhaps the most significant innovation was the introduction of electronic telemetry in the form of tiny transmitters in each car that send a signal to an aluminum strip buried in the track at the start/finish line. This allowed for thousandths of a second timing, removing the human element from timing and scoring altogether. Soon teams found all sorts of car functions that could be monitored electronically in the pits, including fuel levels, fluid temperatures, and tire pressures, and this allowed many midrace decisions once made by the driver to be controlled from the pits.

Too Much Technology?

In recent years, many rules and formula changes have been tried to keep the teams in some semblance of equality, or parity. Various measures aimed at containing costs and making races more competitive have been tried, starting with the banning of turbochargers in 1989. Mandated changes in both car design and track layout (the latter done in the name of safety) have made passing nearly im-

A driver cuts through the rain during the 2003 Canadian Grand Prix. The race is run around an island, and telemetry helps the crew monitor the driver, whose car is not visible to them during much of the event.

possible, resulting in many races that are little more than high-speed processions. Critics, and many racers, charge that telemetry, traction control, and automatic transmissions have turned the driver into a passenger. Others, while conceding that technology has made the cars so complex that no one person could keep track of everything under race conditions, say such driver aids let the driver concentrate on racing. The rising perception that technology has replaced sport and ruined the "show" led to proposals in 2003 to ban most electronic aids and put the race cars back under the command of the drivers. Whether such a drastic measure is even enacted, and, if so, will accomplish that aim, remains to be seen.

CHAPTER 4

Drags and Sprints

Though they are miles apart now in terms of speed and technical sophistication, sprint cars and drag racers have similar origins—the backyards and garages of amateur car enthusiasts who wanted to drive fast. While other forms of racing owe their beginnings to the competitive drive of automakers, both of these types of racing were born of many individuals' passion for cars and racing.

Drag Racing

Drag racing is now a high-tech, highly professional sport that commands millions of dollars in sponsorship and prizes. But it was born in the boondocks—the dry lake beds of California's Mojave Desert, to be precise.

Desert racing raises a lot of dust that can blind any driver who is not in first place. To get around this potentially lethal problem, drag racing became a race against the clock rather than another car. As early as 1937 the Southern California Timing Association was running timing races at Lake Muroc. The starter sent drivers off on a one-mile acceleration run one by one; each time was measured by a pair of stopwatches. This kind of racing was safer, and it gave the participants a more accurate picture of their cars' performance. But racing only the clock was a bit too abstract for some hot-rodders. They took to drag racing in the streets of Southern California.

Like stock car racing, drag racing started out as something of an outlaw sport. Hot-rodders who wanted to see who had the fastest car were bound to break the speed limit. Many street races were spontaneous, or nearly so, and for some, beating the cops was as much a part of the thrill (and of the hot-rod culture) as beating the competition. Racers would gather quickly, have a fast agreement on the "rules" and length of the race, then take off.

Negative public opinion, constant police attention, and the inherent dangers of racing on streets, abandoned airfields, parking lots, and the ever-popular paved bed of the Los Angeles River, stimulated the shift to closed courses. However, street racing had a major effect on the way drag racing became organized. "The racers learned . . . that they could test their mettle and mechanical prowess quite nicely in a short sprint," says Robert C. Post, a professor of the history of engineering and technology at Johns Hopkins University. "So it was that drag racing was defined at the midpoint of the twentieth century. Efficiency would be defined two ways. One was getting from point A to B quickly, and eventually, the primary challenge would become one of minimizing *elapsed time* (ET). That was what won races. But sheer speed counted for a lot, too. The standing mile record, held by a German, had stood for decades at about two hundred miles per hour. By the mid-1960s, so-called dragsters were clocking two hundred

miles per hour in a quarter mile, or 440 yards, which became the standard distance."[12]

The Man Who Made the Sport

Wally Parks, the man who founded the National Hot Rod Association (NHRA), was born in 1913 in Oklahoma, but his family moved to California in the early 1920s. He was part of the desert racing scene in the late 1930s, but World War II ended all racing, and Parks served in the South Pacific. When he came back he became the editor of *Hot Rod* magazine, which gave him the position and the power to create the NHRA in 1951.

On June 19, 1950, the first Santa Ana Drags, in Santa Ana, California, were held on an unused airport runway. Street racer C.J. Hart, who ran a used car lot near the airfield, organized the first meets. His somewhat primitive timing apparatus, a pair of photoelectric cells that activated a clock that was set up in an old hearse at the finish, recorded only top speed at the quarter-mile mark. This set the precedent for the 1,320-foot track length that is the standard in drag racing. The top speed recorded at the first Santa Ana was 120 miles per hour.

Santa Ana was just one of many impromptu drag strips in Southern California. In an effort to organize things and maintain the records the dragsters were

Dragsters race on a sand track. Early drag races took place on empty lots and unused airport runways.

forever challenging, Parks convinced several race organizers to accept him and his rules as a kind of oversight body. This was the origin of the NHRA.

The NHRA's first official race was run in April 1953 in a parking lot at the Los Angeles County Fairgrounds in Pomona, California. Fifteen thousand spectators turned out to watch about one hundred cars. Two months later close to thirty-five thousand crowded Paradise Mesa near San Diego, California. At this meet the timing was impeccable, and there were true standing starts. Speed was measured from sixty-four feet before the 1,320-foot mark to sixty-four feet beyond it, which meant that acceleration, too, was accurately measured. Though

there were still desert races and street drags, the outlaw sport was on its way to respectability.

Early Dragsters

The first hot rods were mass-produced automobiles—Fords, Chevys, Hudsons, and every other make—that were stripped down to make them as light as possible while the engines were tuned up to deliver maximum horsepower. Street racers had to conform to the minimum requirements of the laws, which meant that they had to have weight-adding things like fenders, bumpers, and headlights. Hot rods that raced only on tracks had no such constraints—soon cars were racing that were little more than the stock frame of steel rails, with four wheels, a transmission, an engine, and a seat.

The first dragster engines were the flat-head V8s that Ford and Mercury produced between 1932 and 1953. Toward the end of their production run, they generated one hundred horsepower, and most mechanics could double that without too much trouble. However, the horsepower boost brought the hot rod racers up against two other variables—traction, and handling. Trade-offs between improvements to one, and the impact of those improvements on another—for example, the trade-off between tires that could get better traction for a faster acceleration but that might cut a car's top speed down—have been the entire story of the evolution of drag racing.

Another way to boost horsepower was to tinker with the fuel. Before the war German and Italian Grand Prix teams had experimented with nitro fuel compounds; postwar American hot-rodders latched onto nitromethane because it gave an enormous kick start that lasted long enough to push the car 1,320 feet. Even though nitro was hundreds of times more expensive than gasoline, it became the "poor man's supercharger" in the early 1950s.

The thunder of an engine on nitro became the signature sound of drag racing. The spectacle of the nitro-fueled flash fire (actually the hydrogen in the air above the

WHY "DRAG?"

No one is quite sure where the term "drag racing" originated. The most plausible explanation is that "dragging" was slang for the way hot-rodders got ready to run: standing on the clutch and holding the transmission in gear longer than normal. Often a city's or town's main street is referred to as its "main drag," but that is probably an expression that arose from drag racing rather than being the source of the name. The term "dragster" first appeared in print, in quotation marks, in the January 1953 issue of *Hot Rod,* as part of the caption of a picture of Art Chrisman's "modified"—a single-seater, purpose-built, racer that is generally regarded as the ancestor of modern drag racers. The following month the word appeared again, without the punctuation, and the term has persisted ever since.

A 1955 dragster poses proudly in his colorfully named "Green Monster."

engine, ignited by the exhaust) as the top fuel dragster, or funny car, shoots off the starting line is one of the reasons the main events at most drag meets are run at night. The spectacle is just as important to many fans as the speed.

The NHRA Rules

In 1955 the NHRA staged its first national event, simply called "The Nationals" in Great Bend, Kansas. The Nationals were held several places around the United States before landing permanently in Indianapolis. The Winternationals, held at Pomona, California, became the season-opening event in 1961. By 2003 the NHRA schedule had twenty-two national events, held from Washington to New Jersey and from Minnesota to Florida, and forty-two regional ones.

By the early 1960s, the top drag racers were all purpose-built machines, though

POWER CURVE

Top fuel dragsters generate almost unimaginable power. One dragster's engine makes more horsepower than the first eight rows (twenty-four stock cars) at Daytona. Under full throttle the engine consumes 1.5 gallons of nitromethane per second, the same rate of fuel consumption as a fully loaded 747 passenger jet but with four times the energy output of the jet's engines.

Essentially a rocket on wheels, a dragster must accelerate at an average of more than four Gs (four times the pull of gravity) to exceed three hundred miles per hour in 4.5 seconds. Before reaching the halfway point of the track, only 660 feet from where it started, the dragster is doing two hundred miles per hour and the driver is enduring eight Gs. Brakes cannot stop a car going that fast, so top fuelers and funny cars use parachutes. When the chutes are deployed, the deceleration forces on the car and driver hit five Gs. This is similar to the G forces fighter-jet pilots face, but top fuel drivers experience that five or six times a day during meets.

A top fuel dragster smokes its tires while waiting for the start of a race.

cars in the class called Pro Stocks must retain something close to the original configuration of the American-made car they are designed on. There are more than two hundred classes of cars that can be raced in NHRA, many of which are still classic "street rods." This plethora of levels and classes is intended to make organized racing available to as many people as possible. It has also made the NHRA the largest race-sanctioning body in the world, with more than eighty-five thousand members, 144 member tracks, thirty-two thousand licensed competitors, and nearly four thousand member-track events.

Over the years the top pro-class racers have changed in configuration and design, though they have always had to be built within NHRA specifications. The rules are designed to promote two things—safety, and a certain level of competitive equality. Until the 1980s there was far less money from sponsors and race prizes in drag racing compared with NASCAR and CART. This led to a fair amount of restraint in terms of costly technological innovation, though teams were always trying to circumvent the rules. This technological restraint also conformed to an image that the NHRA clung to for a long time, even with its top stars—that of a group of amateur enthusiasts who spent every weeknight after work tinkering with their racers and who went racing on the weekend.

An early regulation based both on safety and cost-limiting considerations prohibited using both a supercharger (which shoots vaporized fuel into the combustion chamber) and nitromethane; the team had to choose one or the other. This gave rise to the dual classes of dragsters and funny cars; top fuel dragsters and funny cars burn nitro, the alcohol classes run on methanol and use superchargers.

By the early 1960s top fuel dragsters were extremely thin vehicles; the engines were moved from the back of the car, to the middle, and back again. They looked dangerous and ungainly—and they were. Safety and aerodynamics suggest that the engines will stay where they are now, at the back of the car, for the foreseeable future. With their sleek profiles, huge rear engines, and fixed rear wings, top fuel dragsters can put five thousand pounds of downforce on the rear tires for the start.

Funny cars appeared in the mid-1960s. They used essentially the same technology as top fuel dragsters, and were just as loud. They became very popular with spectators because they looked like cartoon versions of regular cars, sporting things like huge air scoops, wings, and giant tires. Some funny cars were designed to rear up on their back tires at the start, then lunge forward, creating a great show. So they were an innovation that had more to do with the entertainment value of drag

DRAG RACING: IT'S A FAMILY AFFAIR

Drag racer Jerry Gwinn took his wife and son, Darrell, along with him when he went to meets in the mid-1960s. "It was easier than finding a baby sitter,"[13] he remembers. Later he was his son's crew chief until Darrell was paralyzed in a crash. C.J. Hart's wife, Peggy, not only ran the track at Santa Ana, California, she raced her husband's roadster until he decided they should retire from racing. Jim and Alison Lee, a husband-and-wife team from Warrenton, Virginia, were fixtures on the top fuel scene from the mid-1960s to the mid-1980s. Single dad Tony Ceraolo taught his daughters how to "wrench," or work on cars, during his short run as a top fueler in the 1970s.

Drag racing is too young for the kind of multigeneration family dynasties stock cars and open wheel racing have produced, though Kenny and Brandon Bernstein may be on their way to establishing one. Nevertheless, families have been deeply involved in their racers' working lives, at least since the early 1960s. This has allowed the NHRA to position the sport in a more wholesome light than it originally had; drag meets are now family events with the generations mingling in the pits and the grandstands.

racing than technology advances, says Robert Post. But the real innovation of funny cars was that they had lots of flat space to slap sponsor logos on. They came along just in time to catch the first sponsorship wave.

Drag Racing Turns Pro

In the 1950s and early 1960s, drag racing was essentially an amateur sport. This was largely due to the outlook of Parks, editor of *Hot Rod* magazine and founder of the NHRA. He thought of racing as a hobby, "uncorrupted by money—money for the performers, anyway," says Robert Post. "A big winner would reap lots of glory, maybe even leave the Nationals in a new car, but then he would return to his regular job, whatever it might be."[14] Even the biggest

stars were happy if they just broke even after a weekend's racing.

The stars of the mid-1960s sought to change that. Racers like Don Garlits, Don Prudhomme, and Connie Kalitta wanted to do nothing but race—and make a living at it. This was hard to do, since at most tracks the prize money was winner take all; the other finishers got nothing for their weekend's work. This situation put racers at odds with Parks and the NHRA.

By this time drag racing's appeal had spread far beyond California, and there were dozens of tracks all over the country. Garlits, Prudhomme, and many other drivers started exhaustively traveling from one meet to another, sometimes racing at three or four different places in one weekend. As the racers' fame grew, track organizers started offering appearance money, because they knew that having "Big Daddy" or "The Snake" (Garlits and Prudhomme, respectively) would bring in a lot of spectators. This in turn made the top drivers more attractive to sponsors. Racers like Garlits and Prudhomme recognized the fact that drag racing was entertainment, and they set themselves to creating a memorable image, both for themselves and their cars. Big Daddy's "Swamp Rat" and The Snake's "Cobra" and "Mongoose" (a top fueler and a funny car sponsored by Mattel's Hot Wheels) became big draws all over the United States.

In fact, there had always been sponsorship in hot-rodding, but it was usually limited to car-related businesses, and amounted to little money. Television changed the sponsorship scene, as it did in many other sports. With the expansion of cable TV in the 1960s and 1970s, drag racing got more television coverage. This, in turn, interested tobacco companies, who had been shut out of TV commercial advertising. The drag racing audience was one of their top target markets—young men between eighteen and thirty-four years of age.

Winston became the title sponsor of the entire NHRA championship in 1975, a relationship which lasted until 2002, when PowerAde, Coca-Cola's entry into the sports-drink market, took over. This is now typical of motor sports sponsorship—makers of products that have no connection to the auto industry find they get a good return on their investment by reaching the drag racing audience. And the audience itself has changed—the NHRA has erased the sport's outlaw image and now capitalizes

The appeal of racers like Don Prudhomme helped to make drag racing an extremely popular spectacle.

on its family appeal—based on the fact that drag racing has been a family affair for a big segment of both racers and fans at least since the early 1960s.

Drag racing has achieved respectability, both as racing and as entertainment. The enormous speeds top fuelers can attain—more than 330 mile per hour was standard by 2003—demonstrate a high level of technical achievement. But speed alone has never been the only motivation for most racers. The excitement and enthusiasm that have driven the sport's participants from its beginnings have helped make it a major attraction to marketers and fans. This combination of enthusiasm and money should help sustain it as a sport and a business for a long time.

Sprint Car Racing

"Down and dirty" is the most common cliché about sprint car racing—and the most apt. There is no other concise way to describe a horde of odd-looking little race cars, each with a roaring, eight-hundred-horsepower engine, hurtling wheel to wheel, sometimes sideways, around a short, dirt track. Though the cars are more sophisticated and powerful and the tracks smoother and better maintained, a sprint car race today evokes the races of the past more than any other kind of racing.

For much of its history, sprint car racing was both a minor-league training ground for racers who aspired to Indy cars, as well as a regular part of the racing season for the top open wheel competitors. Indianapolis 500 winners Lee Wallard, Troy Ruttman, Johnnie Parsons, A.J. Foyt, Parnelli Jones, Mario Andretti, and Bobby Unser all finished high in the points in the U.S. Auto Club (USAC) sprint car series the same years they won at Indianapolis. NASCAR champion Jeff Gordon started his racing career in winged sprint cars at the age of thirteen; though several tracks tried to bar him because of his age, he won many major races in the USAC, All Star, and World of Outlaws series while still in his teens. "It was one of the greatest times of my life," Gordon says. "I was just a teenager and having a ball."[15]

Though sprint car racing is still something of a training series, many drivers do not aspire to any other kind of racing; the level of competition is so high, and the rewards potentially so great, that they feel no need to go another way. In 1968 Formula One ace Jackie Stewart went to his first sprint race while in Indiana to compete in the Indy 500. He pronounced Formula One racing as "the real greatest spectacle in racing."[16] Many fans and drivers still agree.

Cars with Wings

Sprint car racing traces its origins to an oval track race in Cranston, Rhode Island, in 1896. Sprint cars (though not called

LEGENDARY TRACKS: KNOXVILLE SPEEDWAY

The Knoxville Speedway in Iowa, which bills itself as the Sprint Car Capital of the World, is in the heart of one of the nation's sprint car hotbeds, the Midwest. The track dates to the early twentieth century and like many historic speedways, began as a horse racetrack. However, the present half-mile "black gumbo" dirt track was built in 1954. The Sprint Car Hall of Fame was added in 1991.

Every big name in sprint cars has raced at Knoxville, as well as many racers who went on to fame in other kinds of cars, including Jeff Gordon and Al Unser Jr. Back in the days when USAC's top drivers also competed regularly in sprint cars, drivers such as Mario Andretti, the Unser brothers, and A.J. Foyt raced there. The four-day Knoxville Nationals are one of the biggest events on the sprint car calendar. The race, first held in 1961, is one of the most prestigious and best paying, with a purse of $750,000, of which $125,000 goes to the winner. Knoxville features large- and small-engine sprints every weekend from April to October; the weekly contests are considered to be among the most competitive in the United States.

---

that at the time) evolved alongside the larger, faster, championship (or champ) cars, the kind that raced at Indianapolis. In fact, for many years sprint cars were essentially smaller versions of champ cars—about a foot shorter and with a smaller, lower, back end, since they did not have to carry as much fuel.

Most early sprint cars were built from parts for the Model T Ford. Like bigger race cars, they originally had two seats but were narrowed down to just a driver's seat many years before the riding mechanic disappeared from champ cars. These Ford-derived cars became known as Big Cars, and sprint cars of the twenty-first century are their direct descendents.

Sprint cars have retained essentially the same shape since the 1920s, and cars built up through the 1960s have a clean, classic

beauty. That shape actually still exists, but now it is hidden under the broad, sloping, two-by-three-foot front wings and the huge, tilted, five-by-five-foot top wings attached to the roll cages.

Some people believe the wings have wrecked not only the look of the race cars but the racing itself. Others point out that the wings, which 80 percent of all sprint cars carry, make the racing both safer and faster, thus more exciting. There are two reasons for wings: downforce and safety.

Downforce became necessary when sprint engines got very powerful in the 1970s. The front wing holds the front wheels down and aids steering. Aerodynamics allows the huge top wing to push the car down with hundreds more pounds of force than the wing actually weighs. The driver can control the position of the wing from the cockpit during the race, boosting the downforce in turns and reducing it on the straights. The top wing has virtually eliminated slipping on the track and allows faster cornering. This has greatly boosted speeds; it is not unusual for a driver to circle a track at full throttle all the way.

Wings have increased safety because they can absorb a lot of the impact of a crash, taking the force away from the main body of the car and the driver. The kind of multiple end-over-end flips common in traditional sprint cars, which also have roll cages, almost never happen in winged sprinters.

Finally, the wings, especially their huge side boards, help pay the bills. They are rolling billboards for the sponsors, which has made a significant difference in the money available to race teams, especially at the top ranks.

Making 'Em Go

The first sprint car engines were passenger car engines transplanted into race car bodies. Ford racing engines came into wide use in the 1920s and the four-cylinder Offenhousens in the 1930s. The "Offys" dominated sprint car racing long after their reign ended in Indy cars, but there

A sprint car corners around the track. The wings on sprint cars make them faster, yet safer.

was no one dominant engine builder by the twenty-first century. The fastest sprint car engines are 410 cubic inch, fuel-injected systems and are not allowed to be turbocharged. Nevertheless, they put out more than eight hundred horsepower. There are classes of sprint car racing for cars with smaller engines, in a bid to keep racing affordable. Cost is a major consideration, for the big engines cost thirty-five thousand dollars.

One unique feature of sprint cars is that they have no transmissions. To get started they need a push from a truck to get up to the thirty miles per hour they need to fire the engine.

Sprint cars were completely built by hand until the late 1970s. This made each car unique; none was exactly like another. They were built to be durable and repairable, and many raced for many seasons. By 1980 kit cars (a car built from widely available, prepackaged parts) were available, as well as premanufactured sprinters. Many do not last a full season; if they crash, they are often just scrapped. This means that many of the famous sprint cars of the late twentieth century no

longer exist, while there is a treasure trove of racers from the earlier days.

Sprinting Around the World

For many years sprint car racing was primarily found in Pennsylvania, Indiana, Ohio, the upper Midwest, and California. Now there are tracks in most states, and some sprint car races are on the card with major league races at large, paved tracks. For example, the USAC Silver Crown wingless sprinters are featured as supporting events at most IRL (Indy Racing League) races, bringing sprint car races to fans who have never seen this type of race. The Silver Crown is just one of the sprint series that races on tracks all over the country; the World of Outlaws and the All Star Circuit do the same. There are also numerous regional and local sprint organizations, reflecting the enthusiastic nature of much of the sport. However, regulations covering engines, car configuration, and other features are nearly identical everywhere in the United States, as well as in Australia, New Zealand, and Canada. This makes it possible for a team that can afford to travel to be competitive anywhere.

CHAPTER 5

Safe at High Speed

Auto racing is a dangerous sport. It is not, however, a blood sport, as some critics have charged. Racers are not out to kill themselves or other drivers, and race fans who love the sport and the drivers do not go to races to see accidents. But racing is undeniably dangerous. That is one part of its appeal.

The appeal comes from knowing that those incredibly fast, powerful, sophisticated machines are in the hands of flesh-and-blood humans. The cars may be technological wonders, but they are under the direction and control of people who are performing out on the very edge of what is humanly possible. Motor racing's marriage of mechanical achievement and human skill is unique in sports. In any

race there is a very real chance that something will go wrong—and an equal chance that it will all go just right. The machine—or the human—may fail, or neither may. The tension that situation creates, as well as the excitement engendered by the speed and noise, gives racing an emotional impact on driver and spectator alike, which is unlike that of any other sport.

Some people who have followed motor sports for many years say that too much of the potential for failure—either mechanical or human—has been engineered out of racing. They believe that technology has removed both the human element and the luck factor—and thus the excitement. Others believe that lowering the chances that a random breakdown will end a driver's day—or worse—allows for more exciting racing. In either case the fatalism that was once common in racing—the attitude that crashes and deaths were just part of the sport—has been largely eradicated by the safety advances since the 1970s.

Engineering for Safety

There are two routes to enhanced safety for race car drivers: first, car design and engineering; second, racing gear such as overalls and helmets. At first attention was paid to the car, but most engineering

changes—such as lowering the car's center of gravity or improving the brakes—were aimed at preventing crashes, not making them more survivable.

Driver safety was not a paramount concern in any type of racing until the late 1960s, partly because there did not seem to be too many things that could improve it. Even the most elementary changes aimed solely at improving driver safety, such as seat belts, were not thought of until the mid-1940s. There was little concept of engineering more safety into racetracks, either. Walls, guardrails, runoff areas, firefighting

Innovations in driver safety such as safety suits and protective helmets have greatly reduced the dangers of car racing.

equipment, on-track medical personnel—most were afterthoughts until the late 1960s, if they were considered at all.

Until the late 1960s most people associated with racing tended to be rather fatalistic, because danger and the risk of death were seen as an expected part of the sport. "I know if I keep on driving, I'll die in a car, but I want Indy too much to stop,"[17] said USAC veteran Eddy Sachs, who was killed at the Speedway in 1964. He spoke for many of his contemporaries: "Am I afraid of dying in a racing car?" the Italian champion Tazio Nuvolari once asked rhetorically. "If you believe you will die in your bed, then why are you not afraid to climb into it each night?"[18] In fact, dying in bed was reputedly the only thing Nuvolari was afraid of—and that was where he died.

There were periods when huge engineering breakthroughs boosted speeds significantly, but other parts of the race cars, such as tires and suspensions, did not improve enough to handle the new speeds. During these years, most notably the 1920s and again in the late 1960s and early 1970s, there were many crashes, and many excellent drivers died. Writer Charles Fox noted in 1971 that "of the sixteen men who started the 1968 Monaco Grand Prix, eight were now dead."[19]

It was the huge leap in speeds and radical changes in car designs in the 1960s—as well as a marked change in attitude among drivers, fans, and race organizers—that finally made safety the third—and equal—concern of racing engineers, along with speed and durability. The man who focused that concern, and gave it credibility, was two-time (1969 and 1971) world champion, Jackie Stewart.

Drivers Demand Safety

Stewart had been concerned with surviving his hazardous profession since reaching the top echelon in 1964. He was the first Grand Prix driver to wear a seat belt, after a bad accident in Belgium in 1966. The death of his fellow Scotsman, the flawless champion Jimmy Clark, in a second-tier race in Germany in 1968, shocked Stewart and many other drivers to the core (1968 was a particularly grim year; as well as Clark, Mike Spence was killed in practice at Indianapolis, Ludovico Scarfiotti in a rally, and Jo Schlesser at the French Grand Prix; Lorenzo Bandini had died the previous year at Monaco). Drivers believed that if Clark—who never made a mistake on the track—was killed racing, it could happen to any of them.

Stewart launched a campaign for guardrails on Formula One tracks, and other safety features such as not leaving disabled cars by the side of the track where others could crash into them. His courage was unquestionable; there was no possibility that his safety campaign could be tarnished by the suspicion that he had lost his nerve.

ARE RACE CAR DRIVERS ATHLETES?

Racing is undeniably dangerous. But can the drivers who participate in the sport be called "athletes"? Up until the 1960s race cars were, in the words of Stirling Moss, "beasts," which drivers had to literally muscle around the track. There were no such things as power brakes or power steering, shifting gear was not very smooth, tires were not very grippy, and track surfaces were uneven. Most races were long—Formula One races were required to last five hours, and, well into the 1960s, the Indianapolis 500 took at least four hours to run. Most drivers were probably quite fit, despite several drivers' fondness for smoking while racing.

Even so, the debate over whether race car drivers could be considered athletes continued. Scientists have now provided an answer: Yes.

A study published in the medical journal *Medicine & Science in Sports & Exercise* found that "drivers are well-conditioned athletes with cardiorespiratory fitness comparable to other athletes." The oxygen consumption of seven CART racers was measured while they drove on several different tracks and again while running on a treadmill. The drivers' average oxygen consumption, which is a better overall measure of fitness than heart rate, was equal to that of a person running an eight-minute mile or cycling at twenty-five miles per hour.

The advantage of being able to pull in extra oxygen is very critical near the end of a race, says physiologist Dr. Dan Dallaire, who has studied race car drivers for more than ten years. Many late-race accidents can be blamed on fatigue; a driver who is fit is more likely to be still pulling in the optimal amount of oxygen to stay focused and alert.

The physical and mental demands on a driver during a race are extreme, and last as long as the driver is in the car. There are no time-outs in racing. The best driver physique is lean, with good upper-body strength and flexibility. Tests have also shown that racers have quick reflexes on par with other elite athletes. Taken together, the top race drivers are also among the world's best athletes.

"He was able to build a constituency among the people who were part of the expansion brought about by the new teams and the widening circle of sponsors," says former race driver and commentator Sam Posey. "To these people, many of them young, the best part of racing was the excitement and the money; getting killed seemed pointless. If sponsors invested in a driver, they needed to have him stick around. If a family with young kids came to the races, you didn't want them to see drivers killed. So Jackie got his guard rails, and as drivers like Bruce McLaren, John Surtees, Jack Brabham and Dan Gurney began building cars, no one had to tell them the wheels should stay on."[20]

Safety Spreads

American open wheel racing was a bit slow to pick up on the trend, until the bloody and infamous 1973 Indianapolis 500. Despite fatalities and serious injuries, mostly burns, in the 1970, 1971, and 1972 races, the Speedway still operated as it had for years. Then veteran Art Pollard was killed in practice on May 12, 1973. On race day there was an eleven-car pile up at the start during which Salt Walther's car sprayed burning fuel into the grandstand, severely injuring nine spectators. The race was postponed to the next day, but rain forced another postponement. On May 30 the race was restarted after a two-hour delay, but Swede Savage crashed vi-olently on the fifty-eighth lap, again spraying burning fuel, though not into the crowd. Cleanup took seventy-five minutes, but the race was flagged for good by rain on lap 133. Savage died a month later of his burns, and the USAC began to take a hard look at racing hazards.

The first and most obvious remedy was to change the fuel rules. Cars were limited to 280 gallons per race and onboard fuel tanks to forty gallons. In addition, all fuel tanks had to be lined with a rupture-proof bladder, like those on helicopters, and the fuel intakes had to be placed on the left

Guardrails (seen in the background) were installed around Formula One tracks at the insistence of champion racer and crash survivor Jackie Stewart.

side of the car, away from the spectators (at least on oval tracks.)

Since the 1970s race car builders have paid as much attention to driver safety as they have to speed and handling. The invention of carbon fiber, the ultralightweight, supertough material that race cars are now made of, has greatly improved a driver's chances of walking away from a crash. The driver sits tightly wedged in a "tub" constructed of it, strapped in over the shoulders, across the chest, and through the crotch. The rest of the components of the car are designed to fall off in a crash, carrying much of the force of the impact with them. Slamming into a concrete wall at over two hundred miles per hour is never going to be a pleasant experience. But technological advances in both car design and engineering, as well as in the protective gear that drivers wear, have turned many crashes from possible tragedies into nothing more than a wild ride, an expensive repair job, and a sensational video clip on ESPN.

Belted Into a Better Seat

Improvements in car design only help a driver if he stays in the car during a crash. To keep the driver from being ejected from his vehicle, engineers developed better seats and the seat belt.

"I went over this bump; I was doing maybe 130 miles an hour. And I almost came out of the car," veteran sports car

SAVING JACKIE STEWART

Hydroplaning at 150 miles an hour in a sudden rainstorm, Jackie Stewart slid off the track at the 1966 Belgian Grand Prix at Spa. His race car punched through two stone walls and hit the side of a house. The monocoque bent around him, and the tub began filling up with gasoline from the broken fuel lines. Trapped in the car, Stewart waited for the fuel to explode. Then Indianapolis 500 winner and F1 star Graham Hill pulled out of the race and came to the rescue. He shut off the fuel pumps but could not free Stewart from the car. American racer Bob Bondurant also stopped to give aid, and stayed with the semiconscious, gas-soaked Stewart while Hill went for tools to extricate him and to call for help. It took them more than half an hour to get Stewart out of the car, then the two drivers carried the Scotsman to the shelter of a nearby barn to wait for help. In the meantime, the race continued. Bondurant and Hill both gave up any chance at victory, or even scoring points, that day to help their colleague. If they had not, Stewart almost certainly would have died.

Stewart's brush with death drove him to begin a racing safety campaign. Within a year a mobile first aid and rescue truck attended every race, and guardrails that kept a crashed car from bouncing back onto the racetrack began to be installed. Even though he retired from competition in 1973, Stewart has remained a tireless crusader for safety, both on the track and on the highway.

racer Fred Wacker remembers about his first drive in a Formula One race car in 1953. "We didn't have seat belts then. So I came in and told them that I had some trouble staying in the car and they said 'Oh, well, you have to keep your left foot pressed up against the firewall and push your back against the seat. That's the way you stay in.'"[21]

However, Wacker could not keep himself wedged in the car when it flipped off the track during practice for the Swiss Grand Prix later that year. He was pitched out of the race car and suffered a skull fracture, broken ribs, and friction burns over much of his body.

Another American who raced Grand Prix cars in the 1950s did not wait to be thrown out of the car, says motor-sports writer Tim Considine. "Masten Gregory perfected the high-speed bailout. When faced with a sure crash, he would stand up on the seat and jump out."[22] Gregory survived to retire from racing in 1972.

But many other drivers were not so lucky. Rex Mays, a champ-car star in the 1930s and 1940s, was killed in a 1949 race in Del Mar, California, when he was thrown from his race car and run over by the one behind him.

Mays disdained seat belts as too sissy, an attitude that cost him his life. Seat belts were already fairly common in American open wheel racing by the late 1940s, thanks to the wartime plane and tank ex-

periences of many people in racing. Stock cars, too, had seat belts by the mid-1950s, though they were not very effective. That was because at that time, stock cars had standard front bench seats. Drivers liked them, and the flimsy lap belts that came with them, because when the car flipped over and the roof caved in, which was common, they could duck down on the seat. On the other hand, bench seats offered little support in turns.

By the early 1960s the formfitting bucket seat was in use in stock cars, and open wheel drivers were ensconced in custom-made seats. Stock car engineers are credited with adopting the shoulder harness used by fighter-jet pilots; the design quickly spread to open wheel racing. These changes made it far less tiring to drive a race car; being tightly and securely fastened let the drivers focus on their driving. The example set by racers wearing seat belts has been used with success in getting people to belt up in their passenger cars.

Roll Bars, Cages, and Nets

The idea of roll bars seems to have occurred to several types of race car builders simultaneously in the 1950s. Hot-rodders and stockers both saw the wisdom of having something other than the driver's head for the car to land on in a flip. Even the dragsters, obsessed as they were with cutting weight, recognized the need to shield

A driver sits in his top fuel dragster, which features a roll cage to help protect the driver's head.

themselves overhead. In modern top fuel dragsters, the entire driver's compartment is now a roll cage. Small roll bars appeared on both Indy cars and Formula One racers by the mid-1960s and by the end of the twentieth century the roll structure was incorporated into the air intake over the driver's head.

Like top fuelers, stock cars have full roll cages. Their construction is regulated in NASCAR cars; both the size of the bars and their placement are prescribed by rules. The rule calling for a bar down the center of the windshield dates to 1997, when it became apparent that the front part of the roof needed more support. Like many NASCAR regulations, this came about after several crashed cars were evaluated for gaps in safety.

Window nets came about the same way. Never seen before 1970, they were mandated after a tumbling crash in which Richard Petty's upper body hung perilously out of the window. They also act as protection against debris coming into the cockpit.

Helmets and HANS

Until sometime in the 1950s, it was an exaggeration to call drivers' headgear a helmet. At best it was made of leather, and more often than not just canvas. All the early helmets protected against was cold and dust.

In the mid-1950s many open wheel drivers adopted a hybrid headgear—a hard-hat top tied to the head with canvas earflaps. By the early 1960s, however, advances in plastics had taken the race helmet to a form roughly similar to a football helmet, usually with a short brim or attached short visor jutting out over the wearer's eyebrows. Jim Clark, Graham Hill, and A.J. Foyt (with his signature red cowboy bandana) started a trend of covering their mouths and noses nearly up to the bottom of their goggles. By 1970 most open wheel racers were wearing full-face helmets, with a visor covering the entire front.

The hard-shell helmet with nylon earflaps of the 1950s (pictured) evolved into a full-face helmet with clear plastic visors for eye protection.

Helmets were a harder sell in stock car racing. Bill France Sr. wore a leather football helmet when he finished fifth at the 1936 beach-road, 250-mile race at Daytona. But twenty years later, on the same track, a bareheaded Junior Johnson fleed his overturned, smoking car—a near-tragedy caught in a dramatic series of photos. And a 1967 picture of Richard Petty taking a victory lap around the track at Darlington, South Carolina, shows he was without a helmet. Even as late as 2003, some drivers still favored the Dale Earnhart Sr. style of an open-face helmet and sunglasses, finding the full-face helmet too hot and confining under the stock car's roof.

Bill Simpson is the American pioneer in driver safety gear, particularly shock-dissipating helmets. "In a nasty accident, we want the helmet to fall apart," he says. "We want to dissipate the force of the impact. When the driver starts getting banged up, the helmet is supposed to start delaminating and cracking. Any force absorbed by the helmet is [therefore] not going to the driver's head."[23]

That alone does not prevent the often fatal damage caused by a sudden, violent stop. "Sudden deceleration injuries" are caused when the car and the driver strapped to it stop suddenly but the driver's internal organs keep moving at race pace for a split second. Even inside a helmet tethered to the side of the cockpit, a

SPEEDING TO THE RESCUE

The CART Safety Team is one of the most renowned rescue squads in the world. Created in 1984, the thirty-member team of doctors, emergency medical technicians (EMTs), and extrication specialists aboard three specially modified Toyota trucks, can reach a crashed race car within seconds. The safety team often actually anticipates an incident because they watch each car so carefully they notice when something is loose or smoking.

After getting the driver out of the race car, the team speeds him or her to a large, mobile medical center parked in the infield at every race. Equipped with heart monitors, defibrillators, X-ray machines, and patient monitoring devices, Dr. Steve Olvey, the series' medical chief, can treat an injured driver as well as if he was in a hospital emergency room. Olvey and his team are credited with saving at least one life, that of Alex Zanardi who lost both legs in a crash in Germany in 2001. With Zanardi still trapped in the car, Olvey and the EMTs used their belts as tourniquets to keep Zanardi from bleeding to death.

The IRL and Formula One also have safety teams that travel to each race. NASCAR does not, relying instead on local medical resources and the rescue crews of each individual track. Some stock car drivers and team owners are critical of this system, but NASCAR has no plans to change it.

driver's brain can tear traumatically in the skull. This has caused the deaths of at least two stock car drivers, Neil Bonnett and Dale Earnhart Sr., as well as many other serious injuries. The HANS (Head and Neck Support System) restraint, a kind of neck brace that connects the helmet and the driver's neck and shoulders into one unit and minimizes whiplash-type movements in case of a crash, is now required equipment in CART, the IRL, and Formula One. Though it was still not mandatory in NASCAR events by 2003, many drivers nevertheless began to use the device.

Fire Suits and Nomex Underwear

T-shirts, Bermuda shorts, bow ties, tweed jackets—these were racing apparel until around 1960. Then it became the height of professionalism to wear canvas coveralls with the team name on them. Finally, in the mid-1960s, drag racers drew on aerospace technology and started wearing fire suits made from the material used for the parachutes that slowed the fall of spacecraft on reentry. DuPont, the maker of the spacecraft textile, turned its attention to racing gear (and the various other industrial applications for flame-retardant clothes) and came up with Nomex. By the mid-1970s drivers in most motor sports were encased in Nomex underwear, socks, balaclavas, gloves, and overalls, which gave them twelve seconds of full protection from a seven-hundred-degrees-Celcius fire—enough time for a safety worker to douse a fire.

Nomex's protection has been demonstrated many times. In 1994 Benneton driver Jos Verstappen and his entire pit crew (also clad in Nomex) escaped unscathed after being engulfed in a fuel fire in the pit. NASCAR Busch driver Mike Laughlin Jr. climbed out of his burning car at the Homestead track in Florida two years later with his fire suit actually smoldering. His only injuries were to his uncovered hands, because NASCAR does not require drivers to wear fireproof gloves, socks, and shoes like other leagues do. Since Laughlin's accident, however, just about every driver wears all the Nomex they can.

From the Race Car to the Passenger Car

Few other sports have as direct an impact on the daily lives of people as racing does. That is because much of what is learned on the track—about cars, engines, tires, brakes, transmissions, fuel, and even road surfaces—eventually makes its way into the world of the average consumer. Automobile manufacturers use racing because there is no tougher environment in which to test a product than in actual race conditions. Most of the advances in performance, fuel economy, durability, and safety in assembly-line cars were first devised or tested on the racetrack. This "technology transfer" is part of the reason car builders and makers of all things automotive go racing.

Michael Laughlin Jr. crawls from his burning car. Because of his fireproof safety suit, Laughlin escaped with burns only to his hands and neck.

Disc brakes—and later, antilock brakes—were originally developed for race cars. So were front wheel drive, traction control, turbo engines, fuel injection, rain tires, wraparound tire treads, and synthetic motor oil. The nearly infallible seat belts Simpson created for race cars were duplicated for passenger cars. Data gathered by telemetry has allowed car manufacturers to measure the limits of human tolerance in racing crashes, the only situation in which it is ethical to use real humans instead of crash dummies. "Henry Ford began using motorsports when he first founded the company to establish a name and technology leadership," says John Valentine, chief engineer of motorsport technology at Ford. "That is still why we are there today."[24]

CHAPTER 6

Stars of Auto Racing

Champion race car drivers have to be "cool, intelligent, dominant, sober, shy, tough-minded, slightly suspicious, shrewd, self-assured, self-sufficient and controlled,"[25] legendary racing journalist Denis Jenkinson said. Though they competed in different forms of racing in different eras, the six champions profiled here have (or had) all those characteristics. They have all also shown that they are very aware of what racing has given them, and they have all given back to their sport—both in their active careers and in retirement. They all share one other thing in common—they survived to retire from driving.

Juan Manuel Fangio

Long regarded as the best Grand Prix dri-

ver of all time, Fangio dominated the first decade of Formula One. He won the World Championship in 1951, and repeated his achievement every year from 1954 through 1957. Though many of his records have been broken since his retirement (the 2003 world champion, Michael Schumacher, has broken Fangio's record of championships, five, with an unprecedented six championships), his rate of first-place finishes per number of races entered (twenty-four wins in fifty-one starts) may never be exceeded. It is also unlikely that anyone will win championships at Fangio's rate: five in seven seasons.

In 2003, more than forty years since he last raced, Fangio remained the benchmark for Formula One drivers.

Juan Manuel Fangio was born on June 24, 1911, in a small town in Argentina. His parents were Italian immigrants and both tried to discourage their son's early fascination with cars and racing. They failed, however, and by his late twenties Fangio was the Argentinian national champion. Racing in Argentina was unlike anywhere else in the world. Virtually all events were intense, high-speed, open-road races, which covered thousands of miles over different surfaces, terrains, and altitudes, and which lasted several days. From this grueling racing, Fangio learned to drive fast in almost any conditions and to get the most out of whatever he was driving.

Had it not been for World War II, Fangio would have won many more Grand Prix. Because the war interfered, he did not race in Europe until he was thirty-nine. His reputation preceded him and he drove for the top teams: Alfa Romeo, Mercedes, Ferrari, and Maserati. In an era when even the best cars were unpredictable and hard to handle, Fangio seemed to be able to drive anything. His sometime teammate, and the only driver

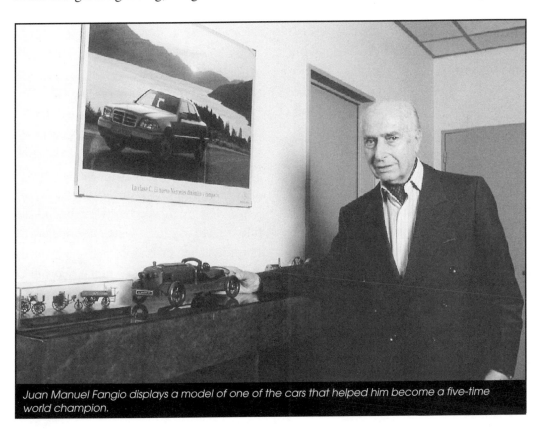

Juan Manuel Fangio displays a model of one of the cars that helped him become a five-time world champion.

of his era generally considered to be his peer, British racer Stirling Moss, said, "Fangio could get into an absolute bastard of a car and draw the maximum out of it, or get into a beautiful car and take the maximum there was in it. I don't care how fast you went, boy, he could always go quicker. No man who ever sat in a racing car made fewer mistakes than Fangio. The man's judgement was just incredibly good, never mind his sheer ability, his strength, his quickness."[26]

Fangio's ferocious driving skills contrasted with his gentlemanly demeanor off the track. In an era of rich, playboy drivers, Fangio stood out by being quiet, clean-living, and faithful to his wife. Like many drivers of his time, Fangio also competed in sports car racing, winning the 1956 and 1957 12 Hours of Sebring races in Florida for Ferrari and Maserati, respectively, and finishing third in the disastrous 1955 Le Mans. After the 1957 championship, he retired at the age of forty-six, having no more to accomplish in his sport. He returned to Argentina where he remained a national hero until the end of his life. Unlike most of the men he raced against, Fangio died in 1995 of natural causes.

A.J. Foyt

A.J. Foyt Jr. is one of the greatest drivers of all time. He won twelve National Championships and was the first man to win the Indianapolis 500 four times (1961, 1964, 1967, and 1977), a feat equaled only by Rick Mears and Al Unser Sr. It is unlikely that anyone will ever match his record of thirty-five Indianapolis 500s. Foyt has also raced more miles than any other driver at the Indy 500, more than twelve thousand. A tough, race-savvy Texan, Foyt has a reputation for being as hotheaded and volatile off the track as he was cool and focused in the race car.

Anthony Joseph Foyt was born on January 16, 1935, in Houston, Texas. He started racing at the age of three, and by the age of five he was outrunning some adult drivers. Foyt Sr. built his son's first professional midget car, which the lad raced all over the Midwest and became widely regarded as the best midget racer of all time. He made his first appearance at Indianapolis in 1958. His car did not finish the race, but Foyt made enough of an impression to be invited along for a USAC-sponsored race at the high-banked track at Monza, Italy, which also included Formula One drivers. There he placed sixth, driving in relief of French Formula One ace Jean-Paul Trintignant.

Throughout the 1960s, Foyt stayed as dedicated to racing USAC stock cars as he did to champ cars, winning the title in 1968. Foyt also raced in NASCAR during that period, winning the Firecracker 400 at Daytona in 1965, the Atlanta 500 in

FAMILY DYNASTIES: THE ANDRETTIS

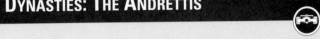

Mario Andretti always wanted to be a race car driver. Born February 28, 1940, in Montona, Italy, his childhood was disrupted by war and life in a refugee camp. In 1954, though, Andretti and his twin brother, Aldo, saw their idol, Alberto Ascari, race in the Italian Grand Prix. They resolved to be race car drivers, a goal that looked unlikely when their parents moved the family to America.

They settled in Nazareth, Pennsylvania, a little town with a half-mile dirt oval track. The Andretti twins began to chase their dream, moving up the USAC ranks in sprint cars and midgets. An accident ended Aldo's racing career, but Mario qualified for his first Indianapolis 500 in 1965, finishing third and winning Rookie of the Year. In 1969 he won the race.

Andretti went on to win many different types of races: NASCAR's Daytona 500 in 1967, and the Pike's Peak Hill Climb in Colorado, in 1969. In the early 1970s he started splitting his time between USAC and Formula One, winning the South African Grand Prix for Ferrari in 1971. After several years of juggling both series, Andretti turned all his attention to Formula One in 1975, joining the short-lived Vel's Parnelli Jones team. In 1976 Andretti joined Colin Chapman's resurgent Lotus team and won the World Driving Championship in 1978, only the second American

to do so. Returning full time to American open wheel racing in 1980, Andretti teamed with his son Michael in a long, successful partnership with the Newman-Haas team. At age fifty-two he became the oldest driver to win the pole position—that is, set the fastest qualifying time—in open wheel history, with a 230-miles-per-hour speed at Michigan. The following year he became the oldest ever winner, scoring at Phoenix, Arizona. In 2000 he was named Driver of the Century by both the Associated Press and *Racer* magazine.

Michael Andretti, born October 5, 1962, ended his driving career at the 2003 Indianapolis 500. In many ways he exceeded his father's achievements, at least in Indy car racing. Michael won more races than did his father, and two CART titles, but the Indy 500 eluded him. His sole season in Formula One, struggling with a McLaren team in a transition year, was disappointing. Now the owner of a highly competitive racing team, Andretti-Green, Michael's best days in racing may yet be ahead of him.

John Andretti, Aldo's son, was a consistent midpack racer in CART, then moved to what appeared to be a promising Petty team in NASCAR. He won only three races in nine seasons, and was released midway through the 2003 season. Michael's teenage son, Marco, is racing karts and showing that racing can be in the blood.

1964 and 1971, and the 1971 NASCAR 500 in Ontario, California. It was not unusual at that time for Foyt and other top stars to race on Saturday night on a short dirt track in a sprint car, then climb into a champ car or stock car on Sunday afternoon on a giant superspeedway. But few drivers were as versatile as Foyt—he won several major sports car road races, and took Le Mans with Dan Gurney in 1967 in the legendary Ford GT40. It is unlikely that anyone will ever match his record of

A.J. Foyt Jr. chats with his grandson A.J. Foyt IV, who is preparing for practice laps at Indianapolis.

winning Indianapolis, Daytona, and Le Mans. In 2003 he was still regarded as the best all-around American race car driver of all time.

Outspoken, short-fused, and passionate about winning, Foyt found that the only race team boss he wanted was himself. He has run his own team since the early 1970s, and in 1996, was one of the first major team owners to jump from CART to the IRL. However, Foyt has never found a driver who can either match his racing skills or stand up to his domineering temperament, so he has never managed to assemble the kind of cohesive team it takes to win races. This may change, however, with the coming of age of his grandson, A.J. Foyt IV, who drove for the Foyt team for the first time at Indianapolis in 2003. Tony, as he is known, was the youngest person ever to race in the Indy 500. He turned nineteen on the race weekend and finishing a respectable eighteenth. The future appearance of Foyts at the Indy 500 seems assured.

Junior Johnson

"Moonshiners put more time, energy, thought and love into their cars than any racers ever will," Junior Johnson once said. "Lose on the track and you go home. Lose with a load of whiskey and you go to jail."[27] Johnson should know—he did both.

Robert Glenn Johnson Jr. was born in Wilkes County, North Carolina, in 1932 into a moonshine-making family. When he was sixteen a raid on the family's home netted the biggest illegal whiskey seizure in U.S. history. Junior had been driving his daddy's pickup truck making local deliveries since he was nine, but he managed not to fall afoul of the law until 1952. By then he was a legend, not only on the back roads of western North Carolina, but the dirt tracks and little-paved ovals all over the South, for his aggressive win-or-crash-trying style.

Eleven months in jail convinced him that racing offered a better life than bootlegging. He brought all the skills he had learned running from the revenue agents—sliding into turns, spinning one hundred eighty degrees, and absolute fearlessness at the wheel—to the track. Still, his career languished until he got a last-minute invitation to run a Chevrolet at the 1960 Daytona. As he suspected, the Chevys were badly out-powered by the Pontiacs. But Junior made a startling discovery—if he got up tightly behind a Pontiac when one passed him, the air suction behind the race car pulled his along with it. (This is now known as drafting, or taking a tow, but it was a new phenomenon in the early 1960s brought about by changes in both race car and track design.) Johnson drafted his way to the front of the field, then shot away to a dominating victory. His position assured in NASCAR, Johnson won forty-nine more races before retiring in 1966.

A consummate tinkerer, Johnson was still regarded in 2003 as one of the best mechanical minds ever in stock cars. Though he shares the traditional disdain for many of the technical bells and whistles that have become part of other types of racing, he introduced one of the biggest technological innovations to all of racing—the radio link between drivers and their pits. In 1966 Junior's car was sponsored by Holly Farms chicken, which used two-way radios to dispatch their delivery trucks. For the race at Martinsville, Virginia, Johnson fitted his helmet with earphones and a microphone. However, in typical Johnson fashion, he became fed up with the constant talk from his crew chief and shut the device off in midrace.

Junior's legend only grew when he began running his own team. His cars won 119 races and six NASCAR championships in ten years, three of them with

HENRY FORD AND THE SWEEPSTAKES

Dale Jarrett (right) rides in a replica of Ford's 1901 Sweepstakes.

It may not look like a race car, but it is. It is the direct ancestor of every race car that ever wore a Ford badge, from the GT40 to Dale Jarrett's number 88 brown Taurus. Called the Sweepstakes, Henry Ford built it for the most important race of his life.

Ford was interested in building reliable, affordable cars for the masses, not just the rich customers virtually all the car companies courted at the time. However, his populist views on the future of cars left him short of money. Despite the fact that he had no interest in racing, in 1901 Ford entered a ten-mile trophy dash, held on a horse track in Grosse Pointe, Michigan, with the idea that winning would attract the kind of wealthy investors he needed.

Ford was so desperate to win he drove the car himself, the only time he ever raced. The Sweepstakes was purposely

built for the race, unlike most cars that were both driven and raced. It was made of cast iron, with a three-hundred-pound, two-foot flywheel. The frame was ash wood and steel plate; the steering wheel a wooden rim with four metal spokes. The car actually took two men to drive it: the driver to steer, shift, accelerate, and do some of the braking, and a riding mechanic, who crouched on the running board and fed oil directly into the engine and flywheel, braked, and leaned to help the car make turns.

Ford essentially learned how to race during the event, responding to the urging of his riding mechanic to keep his speed up in turns. The underdog Ford won the race, and his success did attract investors who eventually backed him when the Ford Motor Company was formed two years later.

The Sweepstakes was believed lost for nearly a century until it was rediscovered under a tarp in a Dearborn, Michigan, warehouse in 2001. The original is now in the Henry Ford Museum in Dearborn, and its restored engine still runs. To commemorate the one hundredth anniversary of the Ford Motor Company, a replica was built and is run at auto expos. The men who built the replica had to also replicate the technologies Ford and his early twentieth-century team used to create the car. So now there exists not only the earliest-known race car but also a record of how it was built.

driver Darrell Waltrip. "Nobody knew more about race cars and how to set them up and make them go fast," says Waltrip. "There was nothing like the sense of confidence you felt when you rolled onto the track driving one of Junior's cars."[28]

Retired with his attention turned to charity work, in 2003 Johnson was still one of the most revered citizens of North Carolina.

Kenny Bernstein

Kenny Bernstein disproves the adage that there are no second chances. After a mediocre career in drag racing in the early 1970s, he quit the sport to go into business. Five years later the need for speed became uppermost in his life again. In 1978 he leveraged his sixteen-restaurant chain for the money to reenter NHRA funny car competition. After two crashes his first year, Bernstein won the IHRA Winston World Championship in 1979. More importantly, he called on two decades worth of business savvy to persuade Budweiser beer to become his team sponsor.

The Budweiser King Funny Car debuted in 1980, and Bernstein went on to dominate the class throughout the 1980s, winning thirty NHRA national events and four consecutive Winston championships from 1985–1988.

At the same time, Bernstein was becoming one of the most visible race car drivers and owners in the United States. He competed in CART, driving the car of his Budweiser King Indy car racing team, and directed the operations of his NASCAR team, King Racing. He is the only race team owner to have won races in all of the top three American racing series: NASCAR, NHRA, and Indy cars.

Not content with that, Bernstein moved up to top fuel dragsters in 1990. He was the first driver to break the three-hundred-mile-per-hour mark, on March 20, 1992. In 1996 he won the NHRA Top Fuel Championship, making him the "Dual Fuel" champion, the only driver to win titles in both top fuel and funny car categories. Bernstein continued to make strong showings into the twenty-first century, but feeling the physical effects of constantly subjecting his fifty-eight-year-old body to the extreme forces of starting and stopping a top fuel dragster, and hoping to devote more time to his growing business interests, he announced his retirement at the end of the 2002 season.

Fate intervened when his son and successor, Brandon, was injured in a crash early in the 2003 season. Bernstein stepped back into the seat and found that, at age fifty-eight, the competitive fires still burn. "If you ask me whether I missed driving and competing, the answer is a resounding yes," he says. "I look at the decision to retire, now in retrospect, and I understand why Michael Jordan, Mario Lemieux and all those guys came back. They missed it."[29] Now one of the oldest men ever to race in any series, Bernstein may find he has in him a few more years at the wheel.

Emerson Fittipaldi

Emerson Fittipaldi is one of only three drivers who have won the Indianapolis 500, the Formula One World Championship, and the CART National Championship (the others are Mario Andretti and Jacques Villeneuve). In the course of a long, and sometimes frustrating, racing career, Fittipaldi's open, genial nature, as well as his immense driving skills, made him one of the most popular racers of his generation.

Born on December 12, 1946, in São Paulo, Brazil, Fittipaldi owes his unusual first name to his father's admiration of American poet and philosopher Ralph Waldo Emerson. (Fittipaldi's brother, who also raced in Formula One, is named Wilson after American president Woodrow Wilson.) The brothers started racing karts (small vehicles with little more than a steering wheel, seat, and engine), a common prelude to a European racing career, in their teens. After going to Britain to race in 1969, Fittipaldi had a fairly fast rise into an F1 seat for Lotus, becoming F1 Rookie of the Year in 1970 and winning his first Grand Prix, at Watkins Glen, that year. In 1972 he became the youngest ever world champion, at age twenty-five. He repeated in 1974, driving a McLaren. In the late 1970s he and his brother joined forces in an attempt to build a Brazilian-based F1 team, which ultimately failed.

Fittipaldi retired from driving in 1980 to give all his attention and energy to the team, his young children, and to his growing business interests in Brazil. But in 1985, at age thirty-nine, Emmo, as he came to be known to American race fans, still felt the fire for racing. He persuaded long-time race team owner Pat Patrick, one of the founding fathers of CART, to let him drive a car for the team, and rewarded Patrick with a win at the Marlboro 500 in Michigan. Fittipaldi faced a steep learning curve in CART where half the races were still held on ovals, but he mastered it. In 1989 he won both the Indianapolis 500 (passing up the winner's traditional milk drink for a bottle of his own Brazilian-grown orange juice) and the CART crown for Patrick.

Moving to Team Penske in 1990, which created the superstar team of Emmo, Rich Mears, and Danny Sullivan, Fittipaldi won ten races over four seasons during one of the most competitive periods in Indy car racing. In 1993 the orange juice came out again as he won a breathtaking victory at Indianapolis, running wheel to wheel with Al Unser Jr. in the closing laps.

A beaming
Emerson Fittipaldi
celebrates victory
at the 1975 John
Player British
Grand Prix.

By 1996, at age fifty and again the father of young children, Fittipaldi decided to call it a racing career and retired to tend to his numerous businesses in the United States and Brazil. In addition to his businesses, Fittipaldi is actively involved in charities in Brazil that aid poor and orphaned children. In 2003 Fittipaldi ventured back into racing as an owner, forming the Fittipaldi-Dingman racing team with a partner. Competing on the CART circuit, the team's future may depend on whether or not CART survives. In any case, Fittipaldi will doubtless draw on both the business and the racing savvy he has acquired over his thirty years in racing to take his new racing team to victory.

Shirley Muldowney

Shirley Muldowney is one of the best drag racers of all time. Not just the best woman drag racer, but one of the best drivers, period. That was always the way she wanted to be regarded. "There is no room for bimboism in drag racing,"[30] she said when she insisted on dropping the patronizing nickname "Cha Cha" in 1973. Though it was an uphill fight at first to be allowed to

RACING ON THE SILVER SCREEN

There have been movies about racing (*Le Mans*, *Grand Prix*), and movies in which races were part of the story (*Rebel Without A Cause*, *American Graffiti*), and movies where the racing just went on in the background (any number of *Beach Blanket* movies or Elvis Presley pictures). Dedicated race fans and film critics alike consider that only a few movies have ever really captured the intense reality of racing, and fewer still have managed to team that intensity to a well-written, well-developed, well-acted story. Race fans point to *Le Mans* and *The Fast and the Furious* as movies that capture the excitement of the sport.

Race car drivers have often played themselves in movies, with various degrees of conviction, and have also often been tapped to drive cars equipped with cameras to capture the action. As television coverage of races has gotten ever more sophisticated and detailed, with a pervasive sense of getting the spectator right into the race car, movie audiences have come to expect that, and more, from race films. *Days of Thunder* also captures the excitement of racing during NASCAR race sequences.

Some famous actors have gone from portraying a race car driver to actually becoming one. The racing bug bit Steve McQueen while he was filming *Le Mans*, and he had a credible amateur racing career for several years. James Garner was similarly smitten while making *Grand Prix*, though he bought a race car rather than drove one. Paul Newman went from *Winning* in 1972 to real-life winning in SCCA (Sports Car Club of America) races. A partnership with Chicago businessman Carl Haas led to one of the most successful racing teams in CART, Newman-Haas, whose drivers included Mario and Michael Andretti, Christian Fittipaldi, and Christiano da Matta. At age seventy-eight, Newman still raced occasionally, and in 2003, was undoubtedly one of the oldest competitors in motor sports.

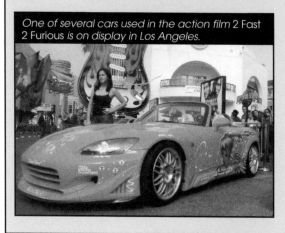

One of several cars used in the action film 2 Fast 2 Furious *is on display in Los Angeles.*

A cloud of smoke trails from Shirley Muldowney's car at Pomona Raceway in 1974. Muldowney is one of the most successful drag racers in history.

race, let alone to be treated as an equal, Muldowney showed the courage, focus, and competitive fire common to all great racers.

Muldowney's life story reads like a movie script and, in fact, was made into a film called *Heart Like a Wheel* in the early 1980s. Married at sixteen and a mother at seventeen, Muldowney's first husband, Jack Muldowney, was a decent amateur racer and mechanic. But she was the better driver, and they just barely missed

qualifying for the 1970 NHRA Nationals. She broke into the Nationals in a funny car, but her biggest successes were in top fuel. She won three NHRA National Championships, including eighteen National Championship events. Her head-to-head heats against "Big Daddy" Don Garlits were some of the most epic in racing.

In 1984 Muldowney survived one of the most violent crashes race veterans had ever seen. Her top fuel racer flipped over at 247 miles per hour after a tire disintegrated. The roll cage, with her inside it, was flung several hundred feet. The crash broke both her legs, her pelvis, and all ten fingers, and nearly killed her. Recovery and rehabilitation took eighteen months, but in 1986 Muldowney came back and raced the whole season. In 1989 she joined the then-elite group of racers who had run the quarter-mile in under five seconds, and was the first one to post under-five-second times at three consecutive national events. Like many of her male competitors, Muldowney (born in 1940) was still racing in her late fifties, finally retiring at the end of the 1998 season.

Awards and Statistics

World of Outlaws Sprint Car Champions

1978—Steve Kinser
1979—Steve Kinser
1980—Steve Kinser
1981—Sammy Swindell
1982—Sammy Swindell
1983—Steve Kinser
1984—Steve Kinser
1985—Steve Kinser
1986—Steve Kinser
1987—Steve Kinser
1988—Steve Kinser
1989—Bobby Davis Jr.
1990—Steve Kinser
1991—Steve Kinser
1992—Steve Kinser
1993—Steve Kinser
1994—Steve Kinser
1995—Dave Blaney
1996—Mark Kinser
1997—Sammy Swindell

All-Star Circuit of Champions Sprint Car Champions

There were no championships in 1971–1972 or 1974–1978

1970—Ralph Quarterson
1973—Jan Opperman
1979—Dub May
1980—Bobby Allen
1981—Lee Osborne
1982—Lee Osborne
1983—Lee Osborne
1984—Fred Linder
1985—Jack Hewitt
1986—Fred Linder
1987—Joe Gaerte
1988—Joe Gaerte
1989—Robbie Stanley
1990—Terry Shepard
1991—Frankie Kerr
1992—Kevin Huntley
1993—Kevin Huntley
      Frankie Kerr
1994—Frankie Kerr
1995—Dale Blaney
1996—Dale Blaney
1997—Frankie Kerr

USAC Sprint Car Champions

Midwest division

1956—Pat O'Connor
1957—Elmer George
1958—Eddie Sachs
1959—Don Branson
1960—Parnelli Jones

Eastern division

1956—Tommy Hinnershitz
1957—Bill Randall
1958—Johnny Thomson
1959—Tommy Hinnershitz
1960—A.J. Foyt

Midwest and Eastern divisions joined in 1961

1961—Parnelli Jones
1962—Parnelli Jones
1963—Roger McCluskey
1964—Don Branson
1965—Johnny Rutherford
1966—Roger McCluskey
1967—Greg Weld
1968—Larry Dickson
1969—Gary Bettenhausen
1970—Larry Dickson
1971—Gary Bettenhausen
1972—Sammy Sessions
1973—Rollie Beale
1974—Pancho Carter
1975—Larry Dickson
1976—Pancho Carter
1977—Sheldon Kinser
1978—Tom Bigelow
1979—Greg Leffler
1980—Rich Vogler
1981—Sheldon Kinser
1982—Sheldon Kinser
1983—Ken Schrader
1984—Rick Hood
1985—Rick Hood
1986—Steve Butler
1987—Steve Butler
1988—Steve Butler
1989—Rich Vogler
1990—Steve Butler
1991—Robbie Stanley
1992—Robbie Stanley
1993—Robbie Stanley
1994—Doug Kalitta
1995—Tony Stewart
1996—Brian Tyler
1997—Brian Tyler

Formula One Champions

	Champion	Country	Car
1950	Giuseppe Farina	ITA	Alfa Romeo
1951	Juan Manuel Fangio	ARG	Alfa Romeo
1952	Alberto Ascari	ITA	Ferrari
1953	Alberto Ascari	ITA	Ferrari
1954	Juan Manuel Fangio	ARG	Maserati/Mercedes
1955	Juan Manuel Fangio	ARG	Mercedes-Benz
1956	Juan Manuel Fangio	ARG	Lancia-Ferrari
1957	Juan Manuel Fangio	ARG	Maserati

	Champion	Country	Car
1958	Mike Hawthorn	ENG	Ferrari
1959	Jack Brabham	AUS	Cooper-Climax
1960	Jack Brabham	AUS	Cooper-Climax
1961	Phil Hill	USA	Ferrari
1962	Graham Hill	ENG	BAM
1963	Jim Clark	ENG	Lotus Climax
1964	John Surtees	ENG	Ferrari
1965	Jim Clark	ENG	Lotus-Climax
1966	Jack Brabham	AUS	Brabham-Repco
1967	Denny Hulme	NZL	Brabham-Repco
1968	Graham Hill	ENG	Lotus-Ford
1969	Jackie Stewart	SCO	Matra-Ford
1970	Jochen Rindt	AUT	Lotus-Ford
1971	Jackie Stewart	SCO	Tyrrell-Ford
1972	Emerson Fittipaldi	BRA	Lotus-Ford
1973	Jackie Stewart	SCO	Tyrrell-Ford
1974	Emerson Fittipaldi	BRA	McLaren-Ford
1975	Niki Lauda	AUT	Ferrari
1976	James Hunz	ENG	McLaren-Ford
1977	Niki Lauda	AUT	Ferrari
1978	Mario Andretti	USA	Lotus-Ford
1979	Jody Scheckter	BRA	Ferrari
1980	Alan Jones	AUS	Williams-Ford
1981	Nelson Piquet	BRA	Brabham-Ford
1982	Keko Rosberg	FIN	Williams-Ford
1983	Nelson Piquet	BRA	Brabham-BMW
1984	Niki Lauda	AUT	McLaren-TAG
1985	Alain Prost	FRA	McLaren-TAG
1986	Alain Prost	FRA	McLaren-TAG
1987	Nelson Piquet	BRA	Williams-Honda
1988	Ayrton Senna	BRA	McLaren-Honda
1989	Alain Prost	FRA	McLaren-Honda
1990	Ayrton Senna	BRA	McLaren-Honda
1991	Ayrton Senna	BRA	McLaren-Honda
1992	Niget Mansell	ENG	Williams-Renault
1993	Alain Prost	FRA	Williams-Renault

	Champion	**Country**	**Car**
1994	Michael Schumacher	GER	Benetton-Ford
1995	Michael Schumacher	GER	Benetton-Renault
1996	Damon Hill	ENG	Williams-Renault
1997	Jacques Villeneuve	CAN	Williams-Renault
1998	Mika Hakkinen	FIN	McLaren-Mercedes
1999	Mika Hakkinen	FIN	McLaren-Mercedes
2000	Michael Schumacher	GER	Ferrari
2001	Michael Schumacher	GER	Ferrari
2002	Michael Schumacher	GER	Ferrari
2003	Michael Schumacher	GER	Ferrari

Formula 1
Constructors' Champions

1958	Vanwall	1980	Williams-Ford
1959	Cooper-Climax	1981	Williams-Ford
1960	Cooper-Climax	1982	Ferrari
1961	Ferrari	1983	Ferrari
1962	BRM	1984	McLaren-TAG
1963	Lotus-Climax	1985	McLaren-TAG
1964	Ferrari	1986	Williams-Honda
1965	Lotus-Climax	1987	Williams-Honda
1966	Brabham-Repco	1988	McLaren-Honda
1967	Brabham-Repco	1989	McLaren-Honda
1968	Lotus-Ford	1990	McLaren-Honda
1969	Matra-Ford	1991	McLaren-Honda
1970	Lotus-Ford	1992	Williams-Renault
1971	Tyrrell-Ford	1993	Williams-Renault
1972	Lotus-Ford	1994	Williams-Renault
1973	Lotus-Ford	1995	Benetton-Renault
1974	McLaren-Ford	1996	Williams-Renault
1975	Ferrari	1997	Williams-Renault
1976	Ferrari	1998	McLaren-Mercedes
1977	Ferrari	1999	Ferrari
1978	Lotus-Ford	2000	Ferrari
1979	Ferrari	2001	Ferrari
		2002	Ferrari
		2003	Ferrari

NASCAR Winston Cup Winners

Grand National

1949	Red Byron
1950	Bill Rexford
1951	Herb Thomas
1952	Tim Flock
1953	Herb Thomas
1954	Lee Petty
1955	Tim Flock
1956	Buck Baker
1957	Buck Baker
1958	Lee Petty
1959	Lee Petty
1960	Rex White
1961	Ned Jarrett
1962	Joe Weatherly
1963	Joe Weatherly
1964	Richard Petty
1965	Ned Jarrett
1966	David Pearson
1967	Richard Petty
1968	David Pearson
1969	David Pearson
1970	Bobby Isaac
1971	Richard Petty

Winston Cup

1972	Richard Petty
1973	Benny Parsons
1974	Richard Petty
1975	Richard Petty
1976	Cale Yarborough
1977	Cale Yarborough
1978	Cale Yarborough
1979	Richard Petty
1980	Dale Earnhardt
1981	Darrell Waltrip
1982	Darrell Waltrip
1983	Bobby Allison
1984	Terry Labonte
1985	Darrell Waltrip
1986	Dale Earnhardt
1987	Dale Earnhardt
1988	Bill Elliott
1989	Rusty Wallace
1990	Dale Earnhardt
1991	Dale Earnhardt
1992	Alan Kulwicki
1993	Dale Earnhardt
1994	Dale Earnhardt
1995	Jeff Gordon
1996	Terry Labonte
1997	Jeff Gordon
1998	Jeff Gordon
1999	Dale Jarrett
2000	Bobby Labonte
2001	Jeff Gordon
2002	Tony Stewart

Indy Racing League Champions

	Driver		Team	Chassis-Engine
1996	Buzz Calkins &	USA	Bradley	Reynard-Ford
	Scott Sharp Bradley	USA	A.J. Foyt	Lola-Ford
1997	Tony Stewart	USA	Menard	Reynard-Ford/Lola-Mercedes/G-F
1998	Kenny Brack	SWE	A.J. Foyt	Dallara-Oldsmobile
1999	Greg Ray	USA	Menard	Dallara-Oldsmobile
2000	Buddy Lazier	USA	Hemelgarn	Dallara-Oldsmobile
2001	Sam Hornish Jr.	USA	Panther	Dallara-Oldsmobile
2002	Sam Hornish Jr.	USA	Panther	Dallara-Chevrolet
2003	Scott Dixon	NZ	Ganassi	G-Force/Toyota

Indy Racing League Rookie of the Year

1996	None
1997	Jim Guthrie
1998	Robby Unser
1999	Scott Harrington
2000	Airton Dare
2001	Felipe Giaffone
2002	——

U.S. National Champions

1902–1908—Chosen by sports writers
Vanderbilt Cup awarded since 2000

Retrospective AAA Champions

1902–1909—Russ Catlin
1910–1915—Val Haresnapo
1902—Harry Harkness
1903—Barney Oldfield
1904—George Heath
1905—Victor Hemery
1906—Joe Tracy
1907—Eddie Bald
1908—Louis Strang
1909—George Robertson
1910—Ray Earroun
1911—Ralph Mulford
1912—Ralph DePalma
1913—Earl Cooper
1914—Ralph DePalma
1915—Earl Cooper

AAA Champions

1916—Dario Resta
1917–1919 WWI–No races
1920—Gaston Chevrolet
1921—Tommy Milton
1922—Jimmy Murphy

1923—Eddie Hearne
1924—Jimmy Murphy
1925—Peter DePaolo
1926—Harry Hartz
1927—Peter DePaolo
1928—Louis Meyer
1929—Louis Meyer
1930—Billy Arnold
1931—Louis Schneider
1932—Bob Carey
1933—Louis Meyer
1934—Bill Cummings
1935—Kelly Potilo
1936—Mauri Rose
1937—Wilbur Shaw
1938—Floyd Roberts
1939—Wilbur Shar
1940—Rex Mays
1941—Rex Mays
1942–1945 WWII–No races
1946—Ted Horn
1947—Ted Horn
1948—Ted Horn
1949—Johnnie Parsons
1950—Henry Banks
1951—Tony Bettenhausen
1953—Sam Hanks
1954—Jimmy Bryan
1955—Bob Sweikert

USAC—Indycar Champions

1956—Jimmy Bryan
1957—Jimmy Bryan
1958—Tony Bettenhausen
1959—Rodger Ward
1960—A.J. Foyt
1961—A.J. Foyt

1962—Rodger Ward
1963—A.J. Foyt
1964—A.J. Foyt
1965—Mario Andretti
1966—Mario Andretti
1967—A.J. Foyt
1968—Bobby Unser
1969—Mario Andretti
1970—Al Unser

1971—Joe Leonard
1972—Joe Leonard
1973—Roger McCluskey
1974—Bobby Unser
1975—A.J. Foyt
1976—Gordon Johncock
1977—Tom Sneva
1978—Tom Sneva
1979—A.J. Foyt

CART World Series Champions

	Driver	Country
1979	Rick Mears	USA
1980	Johnny Rutherford	USA
1981	Rick Mears	USA
1982	Rick Mears	USA
1983	Al Unser Sr.	USA
1984	Mario Andretti	USA
1985	Al Unser Sr.	USA
1986	Bobby Rahal	USA
1987	Bobby Rahal	USA
1988	Danny Sullivan	USA
1989	Emerson Fittipaldi	BRA
1990	Al Unser Jr.	USA
1991	Michael Andretti	USA
1992	Bobby Rahal	USA
1993	Nigel Mansell	ENG
1994	Al Unser Jr	USA
1995	Jacques Villeneuve	CAN
1996	Jimmy Vasser	USA
1997	Alex Zanardi	ITA
1998	Alex Zanardi	ITA
1999	Juan Pablo Montoya	COL
2000	Gil de Ferran	BRA
2001	Gil de Ferran	BRA
2002	Cristiano da Matta	BRA
2003	Paul Tracy	CAN

Indianapolis 500 Winners

Wheeler-Shebler Trophy		Time	Average Speed
1911	Ray Harroun	6:42:08.92	74.602
1912	Joe Dawson	6:21:05.85	78.719
1913	Jules Goux	6:35:06.05	75.933
1914	Rene Thomas	6:03:46.12	82.474
1915	Ralph DePalma	5:33:55.51	89.840
1916	Dario Resta	3:34:17.14	84.001
1917–1918 WWII–No races			
1919	Howdy Wilcox	5:40:42.87	88.050
1920	Gaston Chevrolet	5:38:31.44	88.618
1921	Tommy Milton	5:34:44.65	89.621

1922	Jimmy Murphy	5:17:30.79	94.484
1923	Tommy Milton	5:29:50.17	90.545
1924	Lora L. Corum & Joe Boyer	5:05:23.52	98.234
1925	Peter DePaolo	4:56:39.45	101.127
1926	Frank Lockhart	4:10:14.95	95.904
1927	George Souders	5:07:33.08	97.545
1928	Louis Meyer	5:01:33.75	99.482
1929	Ray Keech	5:07:25.42	97.585
1930	Billy Arnold	4:58:39.72	100.448
1931	Louis Schnieder	5:10:27.93	96.629
1932	Fred Frame	4:48:03.79	104.144
1933	Louis Meyer	4:48:00.75	104.152
1934	Bill Cummings	4:46:05.20	104.863
1935	Kelly Petillo	4:42:22.71	106.240
Borg-Warner Trophy		**Time**	**Average Speed**
1936	Louis Meyer	4:35:03.39	109.069
1937	Wilbur Shaw	4:24:07.80	113.580
1938	Floyd Roberts	4:15:58.40	117.200
1939	Wilbur Shaw	4:20:47.39	115.035
1940	Wilbur Shaw	4:22:31.17	114.277
1941	Floyd Davis & Mauri Rose	4:20:36.24	115.117
1942–1945 WWII–No races			
1946	George Robson	4:21:16.71	114.620
1947	Mauri Rose	4:17:52.17	116.338
1948	Mauri Rose	4:10:23.33	119.814
1949	Bill Holland	4:07:14.97	121.327
1950	Johnnie Parsons	2:46:55.97	124.002
1951	Lee Wallard	3:57:38.05	126.244
1952	Troy Rutzman	3:52:41.88	128.922
1953	Bill Vukovich	3:53:01.69	128.740
1954	Bill Vukovich	3:49:17.27	130.840
1955	Bob Sweikert	3:53:59.13	120.209
1956	Pat Flaherty	3:53:28.84	128.490
1957	Sam Hanks	3:41:14.25	135.601
1958	Jimmy Bryan	3:44:13.80	133.719
1959	Rodger Ward	3:40:49.20	135.875
1960	Jim Rathmann	3:36:11.36	138.767
1961	A.J. Foyt	3:35:37.49	139.130
1962	Rodger Ward	3:33:50.33	140.293
1963	Parnelli Jones	3:29:35.40	143.137

1964	A.J. Foyt	3:23:35.83	147.350
1965	Jim Clark	3:19:05.34	150.686
1966	Graham Hill	3:27:52.53	144.137
1967	A.J. Foyt	3:18:24.22	151.207
1968	Bobby Unser	3:16:13.76	152.882
1969	Mario Andretti	3:11:14.71	156.867
1970	Al Unser Sr.	3:12:37.24	155.749
1971	Al Unser Sr.	3:10:11.56	157.735
1972	Mark Donohue	3:04:05.54	162.692
1973	Cordon Johncock	2:05:26.59	159.063
1974	Johnny Rutherford	3:09:10.06	158.589
1975	Bobby Unser	2:54:55.08	149.213
1976	Johnny Rutherford	1:42:52.48	148.725
1977	A.J. Foyt	3:05:57.16	161.331
1978	Al Unser Sr	3:05:54.99	161.363
1979	Rick Mears	3:08:47.97	158.899
1980	Johnny Rutherford	3:29:59.56	142.862
1981	Bobby Unser	3:35:41.78	139.084
1982	Gordon Johncock	3:05:09.14	162.029
1983	Tom Sneva	3:05:03.066	162.117
1984	Rick Mears	3:03:21.660	163.612
1985	Danny Sullivan	3:16:06.069	152.982
1986	Bobby Rahal	2:55:43.470	170.722
1987	Al Unser Sr.	3:04:59.147	162.175
1988	Rick Mears	3:27:10.204	144.809
1989	Emerson Fittipaldi	2:59:01.040	167.581
1990	Arie Luyendyk	2:41:18.414	183.981
1991	Rick Mears	2:50:00.785	176.457
1992	Al Unser Jr.	3:43:05.148	134.477
1993	Emerson Fittipaldi	3:10:49.860	157.207
1994	Al Unser Jr.	3:06:29.006	160.872
1995	Jacques Villeneuve	3:15:17.529	153.616
1996	Buddy Lazier	3:22:45.753	147.956
1997	Arie Luyendyk (Ned)	3:25:43.388	145.827
1998	Eddie Cheever	3:26:40.524	145.155
1999	Kenny Brack	3:15:51.182	153.176
2000	Juan Montoya	2:58:59.431	167.607
2001	Helio Castroneves	3:15:18.673	153.601
2002	Helio Castroneves	3:00:10.871	166.499
2003	Gil de Ferran	3:11:56.989	156.291

Notes

Introduction: "Gentlemen, Start Your Engines"

1. Quoted in *American Speed: From Dirt Tracks to Indy to NASCAR*, Robert Sullivan, ed., vol. 2, no. 4. New York: Time Life, 2002, p. 22.

Chapter 1: Open Wheel Racing

2. Brock Yates, *The Indianapolis 500, the Story of the Motor Speedway*. New York: Harper & Row, 1961, p. 35.
3. Yates, *The Indianapolis 500*, p. 65.
4. Gordon Kirby, "Unser and Son," *Autocourse*. London: Hazelton, 1985, p. 205.

Chapter 2: Stock Car Racing: The South's Biggest Export

5. Robert Hagstrom, *The NASCAR Way, the Business That Drives the Sport*. New York: John Wiley & Sons 1998, pp. 28–29.
6. Quoted in Hagstrom, *The NASCAR Way*, p. 107.
7. Quoted in Bill McGuire, "Masters of Ancient Technology," *AutoWeek*,

March 10, 2003, p. 46.
8. Quoted in McGuire, *AutoWeek*, p. 46.
9. Hagstrom, *The NASCAR Way,* p. 49.
10. Bill McGuire, "NASCAR Introduces the Nextel Cup," *AutoWeek*, June 30, 2003, p. 33.

Chapter 3: Formula One: The World Series of Racing

11. Giuseppe Guzzardi and Enzo Rizzo, *The Century of Motor Racing*. New York: Barnes & Noble, 1999, pp. 24–25.

Chapter 4: Drags and Sprints

12. Robert C. Post, *High Performance, the Culture and Technology of Drag Racing 1950–1990*. Baltimore: Johns Hopkins University Press, 1994, pp. xx–xxi.
13. Post, *High Performance*, p. 15.
14. Post, *High Performance*, pp. 100–01.
15. Quoted in Bill Holder, *Sprint Car Racing: America's Sport*. Charlottesville, VA: Howell Press, 1998, p. 106.
16. Quoted in Holder, *Sprint Car Racing*, p. 98.

Chapter 5: Safe at High Speed

17. Quoted in Charles Fox, *The Great Racing Cars and Drivers*. New York: Grossett & Dunlap, 1972, p. 109.
18. Quoted in Fox, *The Great Racing Cars and Drivers*, p. 8.
19. Quoted in Fox, *The Great Racing Cars and Drivers*, p. 239.
20. Sam Posey, "Racing's Golden Age of Speed," *Road & Track*, August, 2002, p. 116.
21. Quoted in Tim Considine, *American Grand Prix Racing*. Osceola, WI: Motorbooks International, 1997, p. 62.
22. Considine, *American Grand Prix Racing*, p. 66.
23. Quoted in Richard Huff, *The Insider's Guide to Stock Car Racing*, Chicago: Bonus Books, 1997, p. 129.
24. Quoted in Huff, *The Insider's Guide to Stock Car Racing*, p. 136.

Chapter 6: Stars of Auto Racing

25. Quoted in Fox, *The Great Racing Cars and Drivers*, p. 11.
26. Quoted in Fox, *The Great Racing Cars and Drivers*, p. 100.
27. Quoted in Jones, *Life, American Speed*, p. 67.
28. Quoted in Insider Racing News "Junior Johnson . . . A 'Fairly Successful' Legend." www.insiderracingnews.com/om080102.html.
29. Bud King Racing, www.kennybernstein.com/kb.htm.
30. Quoted in Post, *High Performance*, p. 272.

For Further Reading

Caroline Bingham, *Race Car.* New York: Dorling Kindersley, 1996. Lavishly illustrated with beautiful photographs of open wheel race cars of the past and present.

Glen Bledsoe and Karen Bledsoe, *The World's Fastest Dragsters.* Mankato, MN: Capstone Press, 2003. Clear descriptions of each type of dragster, with simple technical explanations and many color photographs.

Bill Center, *Ultimate Stock Car*, New York: Dorling Kindersley, 2000. Clear, elegant photographs with clear, detailed descriptions of stock cars past and present.

Michael Dregni, *Stock Car Racing*, Minneapolis: Capstone Press, 1990. Elementary, with well-illustrated descriptions of stock cars and how they run.

Ann McGuire, *The History of NASCAR.* Philadelphia: Chelsea House, 1992. Excellent short history of stock car racing.

Philip Raby, *Racing Cars: The Need for Speed.* Minneapolis, MN: Lerner, 1999. Shows the design, performance capabilities, and statistics of a variety of race cars, including Indy cars, rally cars, sports cars, and dragsters.

Tim Wood, *Living Dangerously: Racing Drivers.* Ada, OK: Garrett Educational, 1992. Part of series on risky occupations, this book gives details on the dangers drivers face, and the skills they possess to succeed in racing. All photos from Formula One.

Works Consulted

Books

David Burgess-Wise, *Ultimate Race Car.* London: Dorling Kindersley, 1999. Detailed text, including thumbnail bios of famous drivers, as well as brilliant photos of race cars with important details pointed out.

Karen Christensen et al., eds., *International Encyclopedia of Women and Sports.* Vol. 1. New York: Macmillan, 2000. The history of women in auto racing, from 1896 to Sarah Fisher.

Anthony Cimarosti, *The Complete History of Grand Prix Motor Racing.* New York: Crescent Books, 1986. Race histories, technical advances, and driver bios, year by year from 1894 to 1985.

Tim Considine, *American Grand Prix Racing.* Osceola, WI: Motorbooks International, 1997. Lively, meticulously researched accounts of the Grand Prix/Formula One careers of every American who has raced in that series, from Barney Oldfield to Michael Andretti.

Charles Fox, *The Great Racing Cars and Drivers.* New York: Grosset & Dunlap, 1972. Elegantly written survey of the first seventy-five years of racing, with a strong focus on the 1960s.

G.N. Georgano, *The Encyclopedia of Motor Sport.* New York: Viking Press, 1971. Brief but informative articles on cars, drivers, and tracks around the world, with an emphasis on European racing.

Giuseppe Guzzardi and Enzo Rizzo, *The Century of Motor Racing.* New York: Barnes & Noble, 1999. Elegant, large-format book with excellent photos and detailed captions. Organized decade by decade, with a focus on European racing.

Robert Hagstrom, *The NASCAR Way, the Business That Drives the Sport.* New York: John Wiley & Sons, 1998. An analysis of stock car racing on a business model. Written by a university professor; lively and highly readable.

Ed Hinton, *Daytona: From the Birth of Speed to the Death of the Man in Black.* New York: Warner Books, 2001. Inside look at NASCAR racing, centered on Daytona races, with a focus on the career and death of Dale Earnhart.

Bill Holder, *Sprint Car Racing: America's Sport.* Charlottesville, VA: Howell Press, 1998. Sprint car basics, written by an extremely knowledgeable fan, with excellent modern and historic photos.

Richard Huff, *The Insider's Guide to Stock Car Racing.* Chicago: Bonus Books, 1997. Detailed outline of the basics of stock car racing; a handbook for anyone new to the sport.

IMS Publications, *The 2003 Indianapolis 500 Record Book.* Indianapolis: IMS, 2003. Records for every race since 1911, as well as many other details about drivers, cars, and mechanics.

Leo Levine, *Ford: The Dust and The Glory.* London: Macmillan, 1968. Greatly detailed, though disorganized, history of Ford's first fifty years in racing.

Robert C. Post, *High Performance, the Culture and Technology of Drag Racing, 1950–1990.* Baltimore: Johns Hopkins University Press, 1994. Scholarly, lively, and readable history and analysis of drag racing.

Anthony Pritchard, *The World Champions.* London: Leslie Frewin, 1972. Racing career biographies of the first fourteen Formula One champions of the modern era.

William R. Tuthill, *Speed on Sand.* Ormond Beach, FL: The Ormond Beach Historical Trust, 1978. The early years of speed trials and racing on the beaches at Ormond and Daytona.

Brock Yates, *The Indianapolis 500, the Story of the Motor Speedway.* New York: Harper & Row, 1961. The first fifty years of the Indianapolis 500; an early book by a legendary motor-sports journalist.

Periodicals

Alan Henry et al., *Autocourse*, London, Hazelton, 1985.

Gordon Kirby, "Unser and Son," *Autocourse.* London: Hazelton, 1985.

Denise McCluggage, "Juan Manuel Fangio, 1911–1995," *AutoWeek*, July 24, 1995.

Bill McGuire, "Masters of Ancient Technology," *AutoWeek*, March 10, 2003.

———, "NASCAR Introduces the Nextel Cup," *AutoWeek*, June 30, 2003.

Patrick Paternie, "Reflecting on F1's New Rules," *AutoWeek*, April 14, 2003.

Sam Posey, "Racing's Golden Age of Speed," *Road & Track*, August 2002.

Robert Sullivan, ed., *American Speed: From Dirt Tracks to Indy to NASCAR*, vol. 2, no. 4. New York: Time Life, 2002.

Internet Sources

Cole Coonce, "Shirley Mudowney & Stacy Paul." www.nitronic.com/research/bog.html.

Insider Racing News, "Junior Johnson: A 'Fairly Successful' Legend." www.insiderracingnews.com.

Cliff Kirkpatrick, "CART Study: Drivers Are Athletes, Too." *North County Times*, April 10, 2003. www.nctimes.news.

Websites

Bud King Racing (www.kennybernstein. com/kb.htm). The official website of Bud King Racing includes schedules, sponsor information, and biographies of Kenny and Brandon Bernstein.

Grand Prix Racing: The Whole Story (www.gpracing.net192.com). A large, detailed website describing the history of Formula One, as well as present day racing.

Knoxville Raceway (www.knoxville raceway.com). The official website of the Knoxville Raceway, Knoxville, Iowa; includes a page on the Sprint Car Hall of Fame.

NASCAR.com (www.nascar.com). NASCAR's official website, containing information about all aspects of stock car racing, past and present.

National Hot Rod Association (www. nhra.com). The NHRA's extensive official website includes detailed information about the classes of race cars and a brief history of the organization.

The Official Emerson Fittipaldi Website (www.emersonfittipaldi.com). The official website of Emerson Fittipaldi includes photos, a biography, and an overview of Fittipaldi's race-related businesses.

Index

Picture Credits

About the Author

Martha Capwell Fox has watched auto racing since she was twelve. Formerly a senior editor at Rodale Press, Inc., she has written extensively about health, nutrition, swimming, silk manufacture, and the history of her hometown, Catasauqua, Pennsylvania.